"In the voice of a teacher, this book is a practical gem in the growing collection of resources supporting educators who want to manage their classrooms with care, dignity, decency, and reverence for children at the center of their every action."

— **Carla Shalaby**, author of *Troublemakers: Lessons in Freedom from Young Children at School*

"As a classroom teacher, I appreciate that *Lessons in Community* offers a thoughtful and practical path to align my day-to-day teaching with the belief that all children deserve dignity and agency at school. Moving away from methods built on control and compliance can feel daunting, but this book provides clear guidance and practical lessons that show teachers how we can create a more equitable and caring classroom community."

— **Jessica DiBeneditto**, sixth-grade teacher

"Mari Dean captures the frustration educators are experiencing regarding the ineffectiveness of management 'tricks' in addressing the deeper challenges faced by our students. Mari's approach guides learners to observe and reflect on everyday interactions and then collaborate to find solutions that work for the classroom community. This is a must-have resource for building student efficacy, collective responsibility, and enduring social and emotional skills."

— **Mary Anne Buckley**, author of *Sharing the Blue Crayon: How to Integrate Social, Emotional, and Literacy Learning*

"*Lessons in Community* is a much-needed and practical guide for educators who are looking to build a stronger, more connected classroom community through the lens of social-emotional learning. Mari doesn't just offer theory – she gives educators the tools they need to get started right away. The book is thoughtfully organized with ready-to-use lessons, anchor charts, and interactive read-aloud ideas. The scenarios and students described in each chapter reflect real classrooms and real challenges, making it easy for teachers to connect the dots to their own practice. In a time when SEL is more critical than ever, *Lessons in Community* is a valuable resource that will inspire reflection, empathy, and meaningful change in your teaching."

— **Catherine Giacomo**, National Board Certified first-grade teacher for thirty years

I0894266

"*Lessons in Community* is chock-full of ideas, strategies and resources for how we can support our youth. Designed specifically for teachers of elementary students, Mari incorporates research, additional resources and clear strategies for implementation and supporting our students to be at their best. I truly believe that education professionals will benefit immensely from this resource! Thank you, Mari, for your contribution to education."

— **Kristin Souers**, Author of *Fostering Resilient Learners: Strategies for Creating a Trauma-Sensitive Classroom*

LESSONS -in- COMMUNITY

A Teacher's Guide to Reimagining Classroom Management and Social-Emotional Learning

Mari Dean

Routledge
Taylor & Francis Group
NEW YORK AND LONDON
A Stenhouse Book

First published 2026
by Routledge
605 Third Avenue, New York, NY 10158

and by Routledge
4 Park Square, Milton Park, Abingdon, Oxon, OX14 4RN

Routledge is an imprint of the Taylor & Francis Group, an informa business

ISBN: 978-1-032-85192-1 (pbk)
ISBN: 978-1-003-53294-1 (ebk)

DOI: 10.4324/9781003532941

Typeset in Arno Pro
by KnowledgeWorks Global Ltd.

To Derreon, Josue, and Kimberly
My greatest teachers.

Contents

ACKNOWLEDGMENTS

This book would not be here if it weren't for the kids. In each community that I have taught in I've had the privilege of learning from the most incredible teachers, my students. I'm especially grateful for the kids who bravely insist that we reimagine what school can be. I am incredibly grateful that I get to learn from you each day.

To my Woodburn community: Thank you to all of the teachers and staff who engaged in this work and who show up every day to learn alongside children. A special thank you to Katy Richman for championing this work. Katy, you have truly shown how systems can change when there are leaders in place who value and advocate for what is best for kids. Jess DiBennedito, I am forever grateful to learn from you and for your willingness to think about the hard things together. Sara Kugler, thank you for insisting I outline this book and for teaching me about coaching with deep respect for teachers and the power of a good process structure. Amanda Dey and Jess, thank you both for experimenting with and trying this work out with our older friends. Amanda Manno, thank you for being a photographer extraordinaire and ultimate hype girl. And to Eric Sorensen, my right-hand man in the classroom, I am so grateful for your willingness to live this work and think through the best ways to support kids together.

To my Baileys crew, Catherine Giacomo, Christy Speicher, Kathryn Rubish, Kate Rinaldi, Suzanne Fisher, Teresa Freeland, Tricia Tyskowski, Kerry Ames, Julie Easa, and Ted Cooper. You have taught me everything about meeting kids where they are and the power of creating a deep sense of belonging for kids and teachers.

To my earliest teacher colleagues—Kelly McCullers, Charlene O'Brien, Erin Flowers, Sigrid Ryberg, Wendy Wall, Chrisie Moritz, Grace Choi, and Kelsey Friend—thank you for helping shape my vision for what education can be and for modeling the importance and value of being a lifelong learner.

To my first teachers, my parents, for being my biggest supporters. Thank you for always asking about how the book was going, for reading drafts, and for your unwavering belief in me. To my sister Jenna and brother-in-law Alex, thank you for your curiosity and encouragement about the book and for funding many, many chai lattes to make it come to life. To Maddie Mihalich, thank you for our many writing dates and belief that this book needs to take up space in our world. To my nephews Leo and Dominic, thank you for bringing me incredible joy and motivation to write this book in hopes of creating communities of belonging for your generation. And finally, to Riggs, my dog, thank you for the endless snuggles and love. I am forever honored to have your yellow hair on my laptop keyboard.

Thank you to all of the incredible people at Stenhouse and Routledge who helped bring this book to life. To my editor, Kassia Omohundro Wedekind, I am forever grateful for your deep belief in the power and importance of elevating teachers' voices. You have been such a gift to have on this journey. To Monica Cohen for your incredible design vision for the inside of this book and to Nigel Turner for helping create the beautiful cover. And to Melanie Moy and Samantha Meagher for all you've done to make this project a reality.

And lastly, to the readers. Thank you for your willingness and curiosity to engage with this book. To consider new ideas, push back, innovate and bring it to life in your own unique ways. Most importantly, thank you for thinking about how to create communities where all kids feel like they belong.

Classrooms must be places in which we practice freedom. They must be microcosms of the kind of authentic democracy we have yet to enact outside those walls – spaces for young people, by young people – engaging our youth to practice their power and to master the skills required by freedom.

—Carla Shalaby
Troublemakers: Lessons in Freedom from Young Children

Chapter 1

Introduction

Going into my first-year teaching, I knew classroom management was a big deal. Despite spending only a few weeks learning about management strategies in my graduate teacher preparation course, many teachers during my internship shared that this was an essential thing to get a handle on early. I knew I wanted to stay away from clip charts and treasure boxes but wasn't sure what else was out there. I eagerly ordered and read as many books as I could on classroom management. I was firmly rooted in my beliefs that I would not use any sort of public shaming systems to manage behavior, remembering how anxiety-inducing these systems were for myself as a kid. I felt confident I could set up a classroom without shame or bribes.

My first year was messy. I had an energetic class of first graders and experimented with many of the different strategies I had read and learned about. Transparently, there were many times when I would see another teacher's class walking silently down the hallway, working for their marble for good behavior, and consider if my seemingly harder path was really worth it. I'd pass classrooms where every child was in their seat, silently working, and wonder if that was the pillar of classroom management that I should actually be striving for. And yet, for the most part though, leaning on a variety of responsive, asset-based strategies and creating a strong classroom community of care seemed to be working for me and most of my students. Except for Damian.

Damian was a charismatic, six-year-old boy, who could make anyone in the class, including myself, laugh. He was passionate about football and loved to show you his athletic moves he'd learned from watching his favorite players on TV. While his high energy helped him thrive at recess and in PE, other parts of the day that required sustained sitting and attention were tricky for him. As I would try and read a book aloud to the class, Damian would roll on the back carpet shouting out inappropriate phrases and introducing us all to new colorful language. "This book sucks!" he'd yell as I'd turn the page, hoping we could make it through to the end. I was constantly conflicted on how to respond. I didn't want to engage in a power struggle and yet that reminder to "keep control of your class" and have strong management weighed heavily on me.

Damian was a passionate kid and a strong advocate for himself. If something felt too hard, unfair, or unjust to him, he would let you know. If he didn't feel heard or get the result he had hoped for, he'd often become dysregulated. Sometimes this looked like arguing or yelling, while other times this communication came out as throwing things and knocking chairs over in the classroom. School was becoming incredibly hard for Damian and he was quickly being labeled by adults in the school as disrespectful and defiant. While I knew his behavior was his way of communicating his needs, I was running out of ideas for how to meet them and help Damian learn to survive in school.

As Damian's cries for help got louder and louder, I met with multiple colleagues in the school for ideas to help him. While many of us believed in the idea that behavior is a communication of needs and that our strategies should be responsive, rather than punitive, the message that emerged during those meetings was that those classroom management strategies weren't enough for some kids.

We landed on trying to implement a behavior chart for Damian. We wrote his goals of having a safe body and using kind words at the top of the chart and then broke down each part of his day with three different face options: a smiley face, a straight-lined face, and a sad face. After each part of the day, I would color in the accompanying smiley face depending on how Damian behaved. If he "earned" enough smiley faces, he would be rewarded with a preferred activity. The chart would go home each day as a vague kind of communication log so his mom could see how his day went.

Here's how this behavior chart system typically went. The first day Damian was excited about the opportunity to earn his reward—playing with Legos at the end of the day. I tried my hardest to ensure he got as many smiley faces as possible (unclear myself what really qualified to "earn" a smiley). When Damian was having a hard time, I would try to motivate him to focus on getting to play with his Legos. "Remember, Damian, only two more smiley faces and you get to play with Legos today!," I'd say, almost pleadingly. At times he would get excited about this, while other times he would tell me he didn't care about my stupid Legos. As the days progressed, Damian would inevitably have a hard time during some parts of the day and not earn his smiley faces. This would often lead him to feel understandably frustrated, get dysregulated, and then earn fewer smiley faces. The cycle continued. I got to the point where I dreaded using the chart, knowing that even though it was supposed to be a "positive reward chart," not getting a smiley face felt like a punishment to him.

In my gut, I hated the chart. I hated that Damian, who despite not having his name prominently displayed on a public-facing clip chart, was already labeled as a "bad kid" by his peers and likely was beginning to internalize this identity. I hated that he was seeing his "badness" every day with circled sad faces on that paper. I hated that the chart assumed that Damian already had all the social-emotional skills within him (because the chart wasn't teaching him any new skills), but implied he was choosing not to use those skills and just needed me to hold him accountable. I hated how subjective the chart was and that despite Damian's cries that he needed us to see him and his needs, the chart continued to demand Damian bend to our version of acceptable ways to express needs. I hated that each day his mom was seeing sad faces sent home, not knowing how much brilliance and goodness we saw in him. I hated that students of color and students with disabilities—those at the highest risk of being pushed out of schools—are the ones most likely to end up with behavior charts. I hated that we were failing Damian and so many other students as well.

This book comes out of years of figuring out how to help students like Damian, how to help all students in our classroom communities, and how to help ourselves live in community with students and work toward a different kind of world. It offers different paths for supporting all kids to develop the social-emotional skills they need while simultaneously reflecting on our own teacher practices and beliefs to ensure we're creating nurturing conditions for kids. My core belief, and the foundational idea of this book, is that we, as teachers, can reimagine classroom environments, relationships, and responses to behavior to ensure all students experience safety and belonging at school. Before we dig in, let's take a look at some frequently used classroom management strategies and unpack some of their intended and unintended consequences for children and schools.

DITCHING THE CLIP CHARTS, STICKERS, AND REWARDS

Traditionally, classroom management is defined as the teacher's ability to control or maintain order in the class and the students' ability to comply with the norms set by the teacher. Most conventional classroom management programs or tools utilize some form of reward, punishments, or bribes to accomplish this, though, of course, do not explicitly market themselves with those terms. Typically, these programs purport to decrease behavior problems and increase students' motivation to exhibit positive behavior and engage in academic learning. Other programs claim that they help the school climate and even prevent teacher burnout. And to some extent these carrots and sticks do "work" in the sense that they encourage most kids to comply. But at what cost? Many systems, like publicly displayed behavior clip charts, rely on judgment, fear, and shame to compel kids to behave in certain ways. Students who behave in a desired way get to move their clip up the chart, while students who demonstrate "bad" behavior move their clip down with accompanying threats of punishment and consequences.

These forms of classroom management that rely on shame and fear erode physiological safety, leading to kids being less likely to take risks or speak up for fear of reprimand. These kinds of systems create the opposite of the safe conditions that we know children need to learn and grow. Can you imagine being in a staff meeting where you whisper a question to a colleague and you're told to move your clip down in front of all of your peers? You're then expected to engage in learning, despite the looming consequences coming from your behavioral missteps. How would you feel?

Another popular classroom management strategy is the use of rewards. Sticker charts, marble jars, and treasure boxes all operate on the premise that if you behave in a certain way you will be rewarded for your behavior. Rewards are often talked about as wholly positive, yet many "reward systems carry the overt and covert messages of threat" (Bailey 2000, 229). By saying, "if you do ____ you'll get a sticker," we're also implying, "if you don't do ____ you won't get the sticker," which can feel threatening and activate heightened responses from kids. Additionally, the dangling of extrinsic incentives in order to compel "good behavior" is a slippery slope. If you have ever asked a student to do something and they've asked something to the effect of, "well, what do I get out of it?" you've likely encountered someone who is used to getting rewards for doing things. While often we'll hear rewards termed as *motivators*, author Alfie Kohn warns that, in these cases, even when we use the term *motivation*, we really mean compliance (Brandt 1995). Even positive behavior rewards create a culture of compliance.

Conventional classroom management strategies (both the carrots and the sticks) also create a problematic hierarchy among kids. Oftentimes the same kids are clipping up, getting points, and earning rewards while the other same kids are staying clipped on red and missing out on good behavior prizes. Kids notice these things. They notice who is praised and who isn't. They see the kids who are in timeouts, circling sad faces on their behavior charts, sent to the classroom next door or the office, and all the other ways kids who don't meet behavior expectations slowly get pushed out of school communities.

I remember one day overhearing one of my students talking to another teacher and the student referred to their classmate as a "bad kid." I felt a pit in my stomach. The next day I decided to launch into a text study with my class reading books like *The Bad Seed* written by Jory John and illustrated by Pete Oswald and *All Kids Are Good Kids* written by Judy Carey Nevin and illustrated by Susie Hammer, to unpack what they were saying and feeling. The first day I asked the kids, "do you think there are 'bad kids'?" The class unanimously agreed that of course there were. As kids shared, many explained that "bad kids" are kids who don't listen, who talk back, who don't stay in line. What they were describing were kids who do not obey or comply.

And it's not just kids who are viewed as "well behaved" who internalize this idea of "good" and "bad" kids. Recently I was talking with a teacher who was working to support a student having a hard time at school. She had met with a school support team who had suggested that she create a behavior chart, as is often the first suggestion when kids are struggling. She wasn't thrilled about the idea, similarly to how I felt with Damian, but she felt like she was running out of ideas. I asked how the chart had been going and, with heavy eyes, she shared that the child had asked her why he had to have this chart. She paused and asked him, "why do you think we have this chart?" He responded, "because I'm bad." My heart broke not only for this child and teacher, but because this was far from the first time a teacher had shared a story like this with me.

There's an assumption with many conventional classroom management strategies that if kids wanted to "behave well" or follow the rules, they would. I've heard many adults say phrases like, "well, if kids didn't want to move their clip to red then they shouldn't have done that." These statements assume that all kids have the same ability to meet classroom behavior expectations, without even considering the diverse needs of kids *and* examining the appropriateness of conditions. These conventional classroom management methods also lack a critical part, which is the actual *teaching* of the skills kids need, not just the expectations and threats around them. Many conventional classroom management models do just that: focus on compliance over building skills. They focus on what schools need from kids instead of what kids need from schools.

Tell Me More ↴

To learn more about alternatives to conventional classroom management check out these books:

- *Better Than Carrots or Sticks: Restorative Practices for Positive Classroom Management* by Dominique Smith, Douglas B. Fisher, and Nancy Frey
- *Kids First from Day One: A Teacher's Guide to Today's Classroom* by Christine Hertz and Kristine Mraz
- *Black Ants and Buddhists: Thinking Critically and Teaching Differently in the Primary Grades* by Mary Cowhey

Think back to Damian's behavior chart. In creating this chart and marking off the smiley and sad faces along the way, we were trying to motivate him to comply without really digging into his social-emotional needs or the specific skills he needed us to teach him. We were ignoring our role in creating the conditions for Damian to feel safe and able to learn.

When we prioritize compliance over everything else, we miss so much of what is underneath. In her book, *Good Inside*, Dr. Becky Kennedy describes using these types of behavior methods as "putting duct tape on a leak in the ceiling instead of wondering about the source of the leak" (2022, 75). Too often we aim to squelch any deviance from the perceived norm without taking the time to observe what's really going on and what the child needs. And yes, this approach to social-emotional skills and classroom community is likely a harder path. To listen, to observe, to teach. But the kids deserve it, and we can do it.

ACKNOWLEDGING AND DISRUPTING INEQUITY IN CONVENTIONAL CLASSROOM MANAGEMENT

Let's dig a little deeper. Questioning, analyzing, and disrupting conventional classroom management practices is a good start. But to really reimagine a significantly different way of building community in schools, we must examine the roots and impacts of conventional classroom management, acknowledge their continued presence in our own work, and commit to working toward something better. Author and educator Alex Shevrin Venet advocates for "educators (to) hold two approaches at the same time: dismantle unjust systems within and outside of our schools, while also helping students who are currently impacted by these systems" (2021, 40). While most of this book will focus on supporting the students within your classroom, I encourage you to check out the books in the Tell Me More sections and begin or continue this journey by reading, learning, and taking action.

Any examination or reimagination of classroom management must acknowledge and grapple with the racism within these systems both historically and currently. Let's consider just a couple of the many data points that illustrate the devastating ways that classroom management is often weaponized against Black and brown children.

- Black public preschool children receive out-of-school suspensions at a rate nearly twice their enrollment (US Department of Education 2023).
- Black boys are nearly two times more likely than white boys to receive an out-of-school suspension or expulsion in K-12 public schools (US Department of Education 2023).
- Black girls are nearly two times more likely to receive one or more in-school suspensions, one or more out-of-school suspensions, and expulsions than white girls (US Department of Education 2023).

In our current education system in which the majority of teachers are, like myself, white women, it is critical that we seriously examine our own biases and the ways they play out through our "classroom management." In his study of several classrooms in a public charter school, education researcher Calvin Zimmerman, found disparities in teachers' differential surveillance, engagement, and responses to noncompliance when interacting with Black boys compared to white boys, often citing harsher, more authoritarian responses with Black boys (Zimmerman 2024). Zimmerman highlights how this impact ripples far beyond the classroom walls writing, "These divergent disciplinary experiences in early childhood may affect boys' future attitudes toward school and their academic trajectories and contribute to the school-to-prison pipeline" (2024, 228). Similar research highlights comparable findings with discipline practices with Black girls compared to white girls (Zimmerman 2024). We often hear about children coming to school with trauma, but for many kids, especially children of color, they are experiencing trauma *inside* our schools. Any reimagining of the ways we create and maintain classroom communities must occur as part of a broader examination of how we acknowledge and disrupt harm in schools and work toward racial justice.

Tell Me More ↓

- *Why Are All the Black Kids Sitting Together in the Cafeteria* by Beverly Daniel Tatum
- *Decolonizing Classroom Management* by Flynn Ross and Larissa Malone
- *We Want to Do More Than Survive: Abolitionist Teaching and the Pursuit of Educational Freedom* by Bettina Love

In her book, *Ableism in Education: Rethinking School Practices and Policies,* Gillian Parekh writes that "Education's adherence to the principles of linear development falsely assumes a universality in childhood experience" (2022, 31). Consider the many one-size-fits-all conventional behavior expectations we see in many elementary

Tell Me More ↴

- *Ableism in Education: Rethinking School Practices and Policies* by Gillian Parekh

schools: walking in a straight line, sitting criss-cross, not talking unless raising one's hand. These practices that insist children conform to one way of being are inherently ableist and disproportionately affect neurodiverse students. And as a result of these ableist norms and practices, students with disabilities are overrepresented in discipline outcomes when compared to their total student enrollment in public schools (US Department of Education 2023). Too often in education we turn the blame toward kids, instead of examining the conditions which might be impacting the behavior.

Children who have experienced trauma also frequently suffer as a result of conventional behavior norms and responses. In her book, *Equity-Centered Trauma-Informed Education,* Alex Shevrin Venet writes that, "Teachers can perpetuate inequity when we choose to see student behavior as defiant or unruly rather than a normal response to stress and trauma" (2021, 36). Trauma responses can vary by person, but often fall into the categories of fight, flight, or freeze. Consider a student who elopes from a classroom. A conventional behavioral management response might be to punish the student, further reinforcing to the student that they are not safe and damaging their relationships with the adults in the school. A reimagined response might look like connecting the child with counseling resources, getting clarity on what feels safe and unsafe to them in the classroom, and teaching social-emotional skills to help the student safely regulate at school.

Tell Me More ↴

- *Equity-Centered Trauma-Informed Education* and *Becoming an Everyday Changemaker: Healing and Justice at School* by Alex Shevrin Venet

Far too often it is the kids who don't comply who raise alarm bells, the ones who are desperately trying to bring our attention to the inequities in schools who are punished and pushed out the most. Rather than work to silence or shame these children, we need to turn to them with curiosity. What are they telling us about the methods and expectations that are causing them and others harm? The kids I have taught who have pushed back against conventional behavior expectations have taught me the most about ways to adapt and become a more inclusive teacher.

LEAVING CONVENTIONAL CLASSROOM MANAGEMENT BEHIND

So often conventional classroom management strategies create a teachers versus kids dynamic. The teacher or school system determines what is acceptable behavior, creates the rules that kids are expected to follow, and doles out the subsequent rewards or punishments. While it is important that the teacher does ensure safety and learning for all kids, this authoritarian dynamic of us versus them creates conditions that are ripe for power struggles and environments in which kids feel like they don't belong. These systems imply kids are visitors in our space, rather than a part of a shared community. Many conventional practices come from a fear of losing control and power, but there are other ways to create safe environments in which kids can learn without inviting chaos.

A critical first step is rethinking the structure or hierarchy within the classroom. When we collaborate with the kids to create the classroom environment, rules, and responses to behaviors there is a shared love and ownership over the space. When a child says something hurtful to another kid, instead of the teacher directing them to move their clip down a chart, we can build spaces that teach kids how to set boundaries and repair harm with one another. When kids don't take care of tools in the classroom, instead of the teacher telling the class that they lose a marble, we can create a plan for how classroom tools need to be treated, how we'll check in on our progress, and what a logical response would be if the tools continue to be mistreated. In these scenarios, we shift away from a teacher versus student problems view, to class community versus problems view. We always want to position ourselves alongside and on the same team as our students. Ultimately, these shifts create not only a more inclusive space, but also teach kids useful skills for being active community members.

As we lean into dismantling the conventional model of teachers as controllers and kids as obeyers, it's important that we unpack both the big and small ways this dynamic can show up in our classrooms. This means reflecting and embracing the curious "why" behind our actions and practices. I had a professor in graduate school who pestered me with "why?" after every decision I made. In the moment, it drove me wild. I was a brand-new teacher and my professor's questioning made me feel insecure and that she didn't have confidence in my decision making. As I continued through my internship, I grew less put-off by the questioning when I realized she wasn't looking for a "right" answer, rather she was supporting me to build my rationale and internal compass. Having kids work in small groups? Why? Choosing partners for kids instead of self-chosen? Why? Calling on that student instead of this one? Why? Her questioning made me deeply aware of the importance of understanding our rationale and ensuring our practices align with our beliefs.

This awareness helped break me out of the "this is the way it's always been" idea of school and develop a community and practices that aligned with my beliefs about what all kids deserve in school. It can feel vulnerable to try a new way, especially when the fear of "losing control" has been deeply ingrained in many of us as teachers. Oftentimes teachers will share that they are ready to ditch conventional classroom management strategies, but are unsure about what to do instead. This book carefully outlines the methods you can utilize to teach students the social-emotional skills kids need and includes many lesson ideas to get you started.

FROM CLASSROOM MANAGEMENT TO TEACHING SOCIAL-EMOTIONAL SKILLS

As we leave behind beliefs and practices that do not serve us or our students, we may find that the term *classroom management* no longer describes the work we want to do with children. I prefer to use the broad term, *social-emotional learning*, to describe the approach of teaching children skills and strategies for navigating being in community with others in school and beyond. So, what exactly is social-emotional learning? *Social-emotional learning (SEL)* is one of those frequently used terms that many of us feel we understand the gist of, but we wouldn't want someone to put us on the spot to explain *precisely* what it means. That's likely because *social-emotional learning* is a broad term that encompasses many components and skills. At its simplest, social-emotional learning refers to the skills children and adults need to thrive. The Collaborative for Academic, Social, and Emotional Learning (CASEL) provides a more thorough definition of SEL as:

> the process through which all young people and adults acquire and apply the knowledge, skills, and attitudes to develop healthy identities, manage emotions and achieve personal and collective goals, feel and show empathy for others, establish and maintain supportive relationships, and make responsible and caring decisions.
>
> (2025)

CASEL outlines these five interconnected components that make up SEL: self-awareness, social awareness, responsible decision-making, self-management, and relationship skills.

What SEL instruction looks like in schools varies greatly. For some it might be a consistent built-in part of their daily schedule, while for others it might be a one-time assembly. Research, however, shows the benefits of consistently teaching social-emotional skills, rather than relegating it to an infrequent event. In their meta-analysis of school-based SEL interventions, Durlak et al. concluded that, "compared to controls, SEL participants demonstrated significantly improved social and emotional skills, attitudes, behavior, and academic performance" (2011, 405). In other words, explicitly and consistently teaching SEL skills matters for children and schools.

As you read this book, I encourage you to reflect on what you most want school and classroom communities to be. What conventional classroom management beliefs and practices must we leave behind, disrupt, and repair in order to move forward to what we most want for children in schools? What new beliefs and practices must we imagine, uncover, and work toward? I hope this book will be a guide for teachers, like you, who are committed to creating supportive, free, and just classroom communities.

HOW DOES THIS BOOK WORK?

This book is a practical guide for teachers who want to approach "classroom management" from a reimagined, curious perspective. It's a book that provides teachers with structures and ideas to support kids in developing the skills they need to thrive—socially, emotionally, and academically.

This book is divided into three sections. The first section (Chapters 1–3) begins with laying a foundation of beliefs and aligned actions that are essential to doing this innovative work with children. Too often we don't have the chance to really reflect and examine what we believe about behavior and kids before implementing classroom management strategies. Here we'll really get clear on our beliefs about kids and use that as our compass throughout the book. Next, we'll outline a generative process you can utilize to understand students' behaviors and determine what social and emotional skill you might teach and how you'll teach it.

The second section (Chapters 4–8) introduces strategy lessons for teaching social-emotional skills. This section is made up of four chapters, each focusing on big social-emotional ideas in grades K-6 and the underlying skills that support those big ideas. Those four ideas (and chapters) are: Regulation, Relationships, Problem Solving, and Agency. Teachers can read these chapters front to back or can flip through to find a lesson that fits the needs of their class or individual student at this moment.

The third section (Chapter 9) includes ideas and responses to frequently asked questions that often bubble up with the work.

Lessons in Community is not a typical quick-fix classroom management book focused on fixing kids or finding ways to get them to comply. Instead, this book is a reimagined way of collaborating with children to develop the skills and strategies that will help them throughout their lifetime. It's an approach that puts teachers and students on the same team, addressing problems together as a shared community. This book is about ensuring that each and every kid feels like they belong at school.

Chapter 2

Laying the Foundation

As a recovering perfectionist, I've now become a big believer in trying things out and seeing how they go. This belief led me to bravely (and terrifyingly) try out horseback riding as an adult. One of the hardest parts of learning this new hobby was how many decisions you have to make while riding. Where to look, when to turn, when to use different aids, what to do when the horse spooks, the list is endless. There were days when I wished my trainer would just hook the lead to the horse and walk us around instead, but she and I both knew that the only way I would learn the skills to ride was by getting on the horse and making the decisions myself (with her coaching and support). And let me tell you, it was messy. From losing stirrups to falling off, it would have been a lot easier if she just took over. But she didn't. And I'm forever grateful that she gave me the trust and agency to learn by doing.

While my beliefs around learning by doing solidified over the years, some of my teaching practices lagged. Over time, I started to get this gut feeling that something was misaligned. I'll always remember the day my kids saw the play-doh. I kept the play-doh hidden in the cabinets of my primary classroom, similar to how china or nice candles stay tucked away for only the most special occasions. I had seen what happened to play-doh when five-and six-year-olds got ahold of it. Whether it was mixing the colors (always turning that grayish brown sludgy color like the roads after a snow storm), drying it out, or getting it smushed onto something, it never seemed to go as planned. One day, I opened the cabinet to get something out and a kid spotted the pristine box of unopened play-doh. The kids nearby started to squeal and eagerly ask if they could play with it. "Not today!" I said, but that gut feeling crept in as I closed the doors. I am a big advocate for agency both as an adult and with my students and I believe in my core that people learn by doing, so why was I being so hesitant to release control over the play-doh?

In my mind, I had predetermined that my kids "couldn't handle" play-doh. This was similar to how I previously thought that if I didn't give kids a line order and tell them to put a bubble in their mouth and make duck tails with their hands they wouldn't make it quietly down the hallway. But in reality, the biggest thing getting in

Figure 2.1 *Students explore and create with play-doh.*

the way of my kids being able to "handle" play-doh ... was me. I wasn't giving them the chance to get on the horse and make decisions. Yes, there were times the play-doh dried out, just as there were times that I fell off the horse, but my kids learned how to take care of the play-doh and use it to create. Now the play-doh lives freely on our shelves available to the kids, because guess what? They learned to use it by doing it (and of course with my coaching and support).

BELIEFS

Developing a core set of beliefs around social and emotional growth and development is necessary for all teachers. This book is grounded in a set of beliefs that I hold about kids and teaching. These beliefs have been built from my own teaching experiences, from reading books written by thoughtful educators and by teaching side-by-side with brilliant teachers who understand the importance of building a community where kids feel seen, heard, and valued and as a result, grow immensely. Each time we make a decision in our classroom we can lean on our beliefs to guide us. In her powerful book, *Teaching to Transgress,* bell hooks describes the importance of this as, "to teach in a manner that respects and cares for the souls of our students is essential if we are to provide the necessary conditions where learning can most deeply and intimately begin" (1994, 14). This does not mean that teachers who hold these beliefs and practices have perfect classrooms. Rather, they have classrooms in which kids and teachers work together to develop the skills and community needed to live in harmony with one other. The beliefs that this book is grounded on are:

1. **There's No Such Thing as a Bad Kid**
2. **Children Bring Brilliance to School**
3. **Kids Are Decision Makers and We Must Give Them Space to Make Choices**
4. **Community Is Essential**
5. **Language Is One of Our Most Powerful Tools**
6. **Routines and Predictability Create a Sense of Safety**
7. **Relationships Are Critical for Growth**

As you read about the beliefs that ground this book, consider which ones resonate with you and your teaching practices. What other beliefs about children, teaching, and learning do you hold? Writing your own set of beliefs that ground your work can be a powerful practice and a useful compass to refer back to. In the sections below, each belief is accompanied by ideas for how teachers have put these beliefs into practice. When our beliefs and practices align, powerful change can occur.

BELIEF #1: THERE'S NO SUCH THING AS A BAD KID

Our brains like to categorize things and find patterns. We look for clues and sometimes use those clues to make broad generalizations about people. For example, we might see a kid in the office or a student who "talks back" to an adult and consciously or subconsciously categorize them as a "bad kid." We might not use the exact words "bad kid," but schools have found all sorts of "more polite" language to label children. "Challenging," "defiant," and "disrespectful" are a few examples of language often used in schools to describe children. At times individuals (and the systems in which we work) are quick to dismiss these kids who don't silently comply and who push back on many of the broken parts of our schooling system. Oftentimes these are kids who come to school with intense trauma looking for a safe place to land. In their book *Fostering Resilient Learners,* Kristen Souers and Pete Hall, experts on creating trauma-informed classrooms, pose the powerful question, "How have we gotten to a place where we dismiss the students who challenge us—the ones who, very likely, need us most?" (2016, 115).

Our mindset and beliefs about kids affect our expectations of them and impact their ability to grow. There are many systemic practices in schools like report cards or class list building where behavior is evaluated and ranked, perpetuating the idea that there is good and bad behavior, good and bad children. But there is so much more to children than just the snippets of behavior and choices that we see. Dr. Becky Kennedy, clinical psychologist and author of *Good Inside*, describes behavior as a window, sharing that "behavior is never 'the story' but rather it's a clue to the bigger story begging to be addressed" (2022, 72). It's critical that we're mindful of how we're taking in and responding to behavior, ensuring that we're using the clues we're gathering as information on what kids are telling us they need rather than a judgment of the child.

IF WE BELIEVE *THERE'S NO SUCH THING AS A BAD KID*, THEN WE…

- **Try not to take behavior personally.** We remember behavior is communication. When we notice ourselves making judgments or categorizing a child, we work to learn more about the child.
- **Know what's "our stuff."** This means that when we notice ourselves making judgments or creating a negative impression of a student we unpack why it's triggering to us. We work to unpack our own biases, even when that experience is uncomfortable. What is it about myself and my experiences that's making me feel defensive or want to throw my hands up in defeat?
- **Understand that there is a story underneath the behavior.** We are in the business of listening and learning about the story, not squelching it. We can look at behavior through a lens of curiosity to help us gather more information.
- **Talk about kids like their families and caregivers are in the room.** This means that we're actively working against deficit language and thinking. We speak about kids from an asset-based, curious lens. We do this with kids, colleagues, and families.

Tell Me More ↴

To learn more about the stance of "there's no such thing as a bad kid," check out:

- *Troublemakers: Lessons in Freedom from Young Children at School* by Carla Shalaby
- *Lost at School: Why Our Kids with Behavioral Challenges are Falling Through the Cracks and How We Can Help Them* by Ross Greene

- **Give kids a fresh start.** Year to year, day to day. We're mindful that kids know that we see them as capable, developing, valued humans. We normalize having off days or making a "bad" choice and working to repair or try again. We give kids the grace we would want for ourselves.

BELIEF #2: CHILDREN BRING BRILLIANCE TO SCHOOL

Too often there is a perception that children arrive at school as blank slates or incomplete vessels to be filled. There is a pressure to get kids ready for "real life," as if the life they are living right now is not yet real or valid. This idea is often further perpetuated in schools as we analyze data and focus on how much of a "gap" there is to fill for a child to be considered on grade level. This positioning can lead to a deficit mindset where kids' strengths and identities can get lost. It's important that we remember that kids are brilliant and whole just as they are, *even* when they're having a hard time.

In her book, *Being the Change: Lessons and Strategies to Teach Social Comprehension,* Sara K. Ahmed asserts that it's our obligation to help kids feel heard, understood, and visible just as they are (2018). She gives suggestions to "help shine a light on who they [students] are: their hopes and dreams, talents, family histories, how they identify culturally, the languages they speak, how they learn best, the story of their names, what they can teach us" (Ahmed 2018, 2). As we take the time to learn more about our students, we can see the assets they bring from themselves, their families, and their communities and integrate those funds of knowledge (Moll et al. 1992) into the classroom community.

IF WE BELIEVE *CHILDREN BRING BRILLIANCE TO SCHOOL*, THEN WE...

- **Observe kids.** Take the time to watch kids throughout the day. We can learn so much about who our students are by watching how they interact with one another, what they're drawn to, and how they approach different situations. In their book, *Parents and Teachers Working Together,* Carol Davis and Alice Yang write that "in order to teach children well, we have to know them" (2005, 9). When kids feel that we are interested in them and see them for their strengths, they are much more likely to learn.

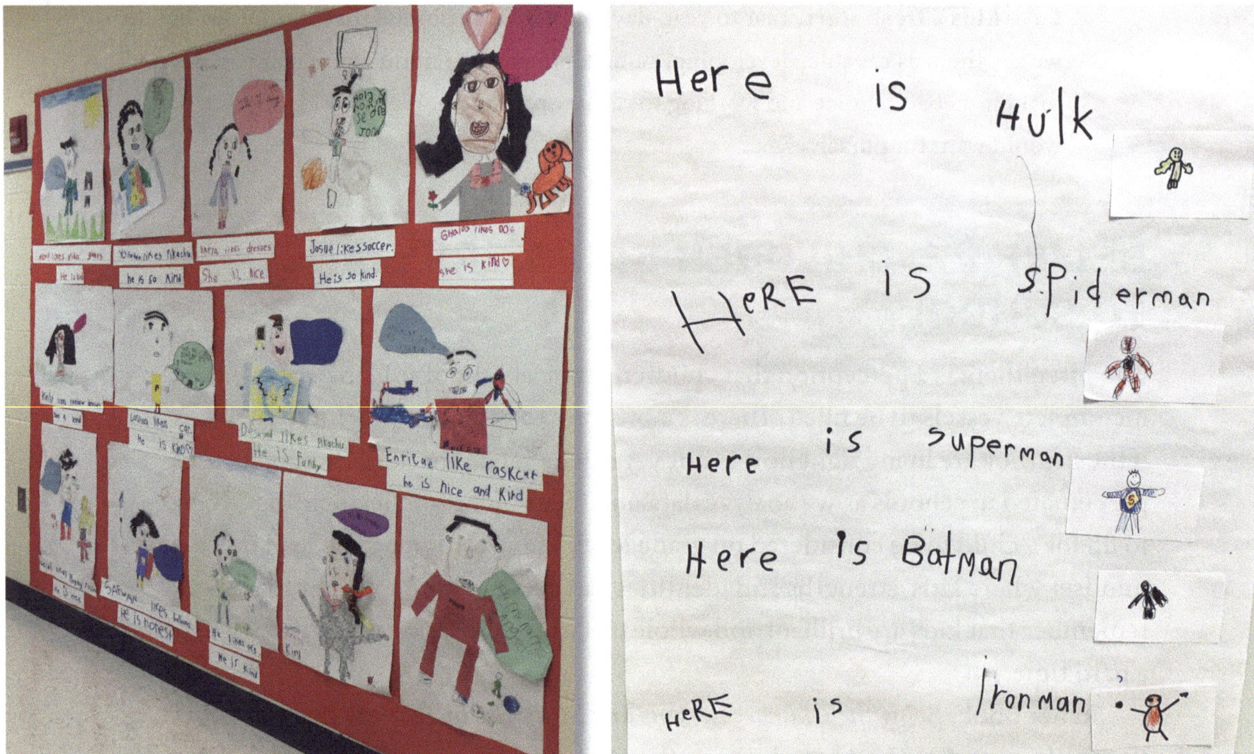

Figure 2.2 *When we believe that children bring brilliance to school, we honor and celebrate who they are and what they love. A hallway display (left) of student-created self-portraits is accompanied by shared writing (underneath each portrait) about what each student likes. Another display (right) celebrates an interactive writing poem created by a class that loves superheroes.*

Tell Me More

To learn more about exploring identities and building social comprehension skills, check out:

- *Being the Change: Lessons and Strategies to Teach Social Comprehension* by Sara K. Ahmed

To discover how to create identity-affirming classroom environments check out:

- *Identity Affirming Classrooms: Spaces That Center Humanity* by Erica Buchanan Rivera

- **Build on strengths and interests.** We are all looking for connection and to feel like someone sees us as we are. One year a colleague was struggling with the loud volume level in her class and nothing she was trying seemed to be making an impact. She decided to leverage a relatable and highly interesting topic, soccer, as a guide. The class collaboratively determined volume levels (huddle voice, passing voice, GOAL voice) and put them into action. This connection not only felt more relatable to the kids, but also showed them that their teacher saw them and knew what they cared about.

BELIEF #3: KIDS ARE DECISION MAKERS AND WE MUST GIVE THEM SPACE TO MAKE CHOICES

Have you ever heard a teacher describe an idea or practice and then heard another teacher immediately respond that their kids "can't handle doing that." Losing control and the resulting potential chaos is a deeply rooted fear for many educators. And to some extent, this makes sense! Our school structure of having one teacher responsible for twenty or thirty children does require structure. But too often, a desire for structure morphs into a tightly controlled environment in which there is little space for students to make choices or hold agency. Many practices like line order, assigned seating, and passing things out instead of letting kids get materials, come from a desire for structure and a fear of losing control. And none of these routines are horrible in themselves. Passing out papers is not going to eliminate a child's sense of agency in school on its own. But it's worth taking note of what we control in our classrooms and asking ourselves if we can create structures and routines that let kids take the lead and build both independence and community collaboration at the same time.

It has taken years of witnessing kids learn to do things independently to solidify my belief that kids learn by doing. I've developed confidence in the idea that kids can take on much more than we often give them credit for by standing back a little at times to let them figure things out and, at times, teaching and coaching into their independence. It might be a little messy at first and they might not get it at the first try, but I've seen how kids can navigate decision making when given the opportunity and support. Alfie Kohn, author and advocate for families and educators writes, "the way a child learns how to make decisions is by making decisions, not by following directions" (Kohn 1993). If our hope is for kids to become responsible, thoughtful decision makers, then we need to let them make decisions.

Children can do the things we often do for them—figuring out a way to line up for recess without pushing or knocking anyone over, sharing a toy car that two children are both grabbing for, setting themselves up for writing time by getting their writing folder, choosing paper, and deciding on a writing spot all on their own. When we give kids the chance to make decisions and coach them through road bumps, they build confidence, independence, and feel successful.

Figure 2.3 *A student uses a Ways to Share chart to support their decision making with a peer.*

IF WE BELIEVE *KIDS ARE DECISION MAKERS AND WE MUST GIVE THEM SPACE TO MAKE CHOICES*, THEN WE...

- **Focus on process over product.** When we focus heavily on the product over the process, we tend to want to control the steps and decisions kids make in an effort to ensure the resulting product is "perfect." When we instead focus on the process and the child's learning within the process, we help strengthen kids' decision making, problem solving, and creativity skills (and so much more!).
- **Build in daily opportunities for kids to try out the skills they're learning.** Whether it's picking out the toy they want to play with, deciding where to sit in the room, or picking out the books they want to read from the classroom library, kids need the opportunity to try out making decisions. The more opportunities kids have to use the skills we teach them with coaching and support, the more prepared they'll

Figure 2.4 *A student chooses her own books in the classroom library.*

be to make thoughtful decisions on their own. It can be helpful to reflect on what skill you're teaching children and consider how many different opportunities in the day they have to try out the skill.

- **Make materials accessible to kids.** Kids can learn so much about decision making and independence by having materials readily available and accessible to them on their level. This might look like putting toys and tools at their level and teaching them how to get them out, use them, and clean them up. This process embeds choice while also instilling a sense of ownership in the classroom.

- **Lean into the messiness.** The play-doh colors will inevitably get mixed together. Someone will cry about being cut in line. A puzzle piece will likely go missing. But the reward of giving children the opportunities to build their decision-making skills far outweighs the benefits of a pristine box of play-doh on a shelf.

Tell Me More

To learn more about how you can set up a kid-centered classroom space, I highly recommend checking out:

- *Kids 1st from Day 1: A Teacher's Guide to Today's Classroom* by Christine Hertz and Kristine Mraz

BELIEF #4: COMMUNITY IS ESSENTIAL

When I reflect on the most impactful educators I know, a common factor among all of them is their ability to create and sustain a strong class community. Kristin Van Marter Souers and Pete Hall describe creating an environment like this as a "safe nest for students so that they learn and thrive and, when they eventually fly, they soar" (2018, 9). As educators, we have the incredibly important job of building a nest that serves as a nurturing environment that provides both physical and emotional safety, a place where kids can take risks and know that they will not be pushed out, but rather nurtured and loved.

Part of building that safe and welcoming community includes valuing and incorporating children's communities outside of school. In the foreword to *Nourishing Caregiver Collaborations* by Nawal Qarooni, Cornelius Minor writes, "All children come to us with a universe of experiences and insight that they have grown alongside their caregivers" (Qarooni 2024, 3). It's our job to not only create a safe environment where children feel comfortable bringing their experiences into the classroom, but also to invite their stories and voices in. What languages, cultures, traditions, and practices do our children and their families have that we can learn about and weave into our classrooms?

IF WE BELIEVE *COMMUNITY IS ESSENTIAL*, THEN WE...

- **Keep the classroom the class's room.** This often looks like bare walls at the beginning of the year waiting to be filled with co-created charts, student creations, and pictures of the kids and their families. When kids are included in the set-up, design, and maintenance of the classroom, there's often a sense of shared ownership and responsibility.

- **Collaboratively establish shared values.** Similar to walking into an already completely decorated classroom, entering a space with pre-established rules creates a dynamic where the rules are teacher-centered, meaning the teacher is the one who creates and upholds the rules. When we take the time to collaboratively construct shared values with kids and practice how we live into those values, the community is anchored by that set of beliefs. If a value your community holds is to take care of each other and you notice students aren't doing that, it's the class community's responsibility to work to get back in alignment with those values. This might mean teaching kids how to notice and speak up when our actions stray from our values and problem-solving ways to get back in alignment.

Figure 2.5 *A group of students works together to create a town while sharing a variety of materials.*

Figure 2.6 *A class promise created by students.*

- **Teach kids to talk directly to each other, not through us.** We've all had kids come up to us and share about how a kid did something they didn't like to them. Situations like this often arise when there are pre-established rules and kids see the teacher as the enforcer of these rules. As teachers, we have a choice to either perpetuate this role as enforcer *or* to support the children in using the shared values as their reference for how to be in the community. This might look like encouraging and supporting two kids who are frustrated with each other to sit down and talk through what they are feeling and need.

- **Pay attention to our language.** Sara K. Ahmed writes about the importance of decentering our normal and being mindful of the lens from which we see the world (from our own experiences) (2018). Ensuring students from all communities feel safe and valued requires us to "pay attention to the language we use and how it can position people, customs, food, or traditions outside of what we view to be normal" (Ahmed 2018, xxix).

- **Take the time to learn from our kids and their families.** Welcome Walks, home visits, or attending events in the community are all great ways to learn more about your students and their families. Listening conferences, where the teacher's role is to listen and learn from the families, provide teachers with the opportunity to learn more about the student from the people who know them best. They also help establish a relationship in which the teacher is not the sole transmitter of information, but rather a participant, alongside caregivers, in a collaborative back-and-forth.

Tell Me More ↴

To learn more about building a classroom community check out:

- *Teaching Children to Care: Classroom Management for Ethical and Academic Growth* by Ruth Sidney Charney

If you're interested in learning more about listening conferences or other ways to bridge school and home, check out:

- *Parents and Teachers Working Together* by Carol Savis and Alice Yang

BELIEF #5: LANGUAGE IS ONE OF OUR MOST POWERFUL TOOLS

How we talk to kids matters. In *The Power of Our Words,* Paula Denton writes, "what we say to others can deeply affect their sense of who they are and who they might become" (2007, 3). The words we choose and our tone with kids, especially in times of heightened emotions and dysregulation, can strengthen a relationship or tear it apart. Our language has a huge impact on our relationship with kids.

IF WE BELIEVE *LANGUAGE IS ONE OF OUR MOST POWERFUL TOOLS* THEN WE...

- **Are mindful of our tone and body language.** We want to model effective communication for kids which goes beyond just the words that we say. This is especially important when a kid is in crisis or having a hard time. We can model regulation for kids by keeping a calm tone and getting down on their level. We want to ensure our body and tone are unthreatening and approachable.
- **Keep our language lean.** No one likes a lecture, and our message can easily get lost in a rambling of words. When we talk to kids we want our language to be concise. We can do this by choosing one point and avoiding going overboard on other feedback and directions. Instead of, "we don't run in the hallways, you know that" we can simply say, "walk."
- **Ensure your actions match your words.** Our words lose meaning when they don't align with our actions. If we say we're going to do something, it's critical that we follow through to the best of our abilities. This helps kids trust what we say.
- **Err on the side of listening.** Too often we jump to problem solving or reacting before taking the time to listen to people. In many cases, one of the most powerful ways to diffuse a situation is to pause and empathetically listen. In *Good Inside,* Kennedy describes this phenomenon: "as soon as we feel truly seen in our experience and our desires, we can let our guard down—after all, as humans, we are less invested in any specific decision than we are in feeling seen" (2022, 22).

Tell Me More ↴

For resources on revising and refining our teacher language, check out:

- *The Power of Our Words: Teacher Language That Helps Children Learn* by Paula Denton
- *Choice Words: How Our Language Affects Children's Learning* by Peter Johnston

Responsive Classroom also has ample resources to support teachers in developing thoughtful reinforcing, reminding, and redirecting language.

BELIEF #6: ROUTINES AND PREDICTABILITY CREATE A SENSE OF SAFETY

Setting up routines and predictable structures with your kids from day one helps students know what to anticipate each day. This helps them build confidence and independence as they know what to do and feel successful doing it. Our confirmation that a routine is well taught and ingrained in the classroom community is when the kids can do it seamlessly on their own. When the class has a shared understanding of what the routine is and why we do it, they can also help support each other in doing it. For example, we have a bathroom stop sign in my classroom that helps people know if someone is in the class bathroom. If someone forgets to turn the stop sign, you might hear another student gently say, "Don't forget to turn the sign so the next person knows they can go in!" This is yet another example of the kids taking responsibility for the routines in the community, rather than myself as the teacher needing to remind and enforce them.

IF WE BELIEVE *ROUTINES AND PREDICTABILITY CREATE A SENSE OF SAFETY* THEN WE...

- **Include kids in creating routines.** Consider how you might include kids in the decision-making process for routines and procedures. Asking questions like, "How might we get ready for writing?" or "What do we need to remember when we're packing up for dismissal" can give kids more ownership over the somewhat mundane, but very much necessary parts of school life.

- **Establish and practice routines as a class community.** Utilizing strategies like interactive modeling to help explicitly teach and practice routines helps students feel confident to do them independently. Some routines we might teach are how to get out and use materials, how to return materials, how to work independently, how to work with a partner, etc. A sign you might want to revisit a routine is when kids come to you asking what to do next or where something is.

- **Utilize tools like visual schedules, timers, and songs.** Kids (and adults!) are often desperate for autonomy and control. Visual schedules and timers can help kids have a sense of control in understanding the sequence of their day. Timers can also help break up parts of a day into manageable chunks for kids. Utilizing songs for transitions can also help make what might be a chaotic unstructured time feel calming and predictable.

- **Revise (don't give up) when something isn't working.** It's normal for a routine to need revisiting or tweaking throughout the year. During our phonics instruction, my kindergarteners have bags that hold whiteboards, makers, charts, and erasers. Bumps inevitably arise when kids doodle on the whiteboards or forget to put the caps on the markers. Instead of saying "no more bags!," we slow down, revisit the routine and revise the steps as needed.

Figure 2.7 *A morning jobs chart that children can refer back to as they independently work through the arrival routine.*

Figure 2.8 *Students use a sand timer to help keep track of how much time they have left to play.*

BELIEF #7: RELATIONSHIPS ARE CRITICAL FOR GROWTH

If you've attended any sort of professional development as a teacher, you've likely heard about the importance of building relationships with kids. Child psychiatrist James Comer famously said that "no significant learning occurs without a significant relationship." Kids who feel like their teachers know and care about them are more likely to come to school, take risks, and learn. When we talk about relationships, it's often suggested to teachers to have lunch bunches or do special activities with kids to get to know them. While these can be helpful ways to bond with kids, it's our day-to-day actions and behaviors that truly build and sustain these relationships.

IF WE BELIEVE *RELATIONSHIPS ARE CRITICAL FOR GROWTH* THEN WE...

- **Trust kids.** Trust is a critical part in relationships. We can show kids we trust them by giving them opportunities to make decisions and try things out, by giving them the benefit of the doubt, and by conveying that we believe in them.

- **Be brave enough to repair.** Positioning teachers as all-knowing holders of knowledge has set many educators up to fear admitting to and repairing mistakes. I remember one day I raised my voice at my class. This was not a common practice and my students quickly became silent. I could tell it startled them. I wanted to push this moment under the rug, but I knew I needed to repair, just as I would hope that they would. My students embraced my apology with warmth and lots of "it's okay!" and even an adorable "maybe you can take some breaths at the break spot." Modeling repair in relationships also helps kids see this process as something they can do with people in their life.

- **Model healthy boundaries.** Kennedy says that boundaries are "not what we tell kids *not* to do; boundaries are what we tell kids we *will* do" (2022, 30). Many well-intentioned teachers fear that kids think they're mean or won't like them because they follow through with a consequence. It can be helpful to reimagine boundary setting as actually creating comfort and safety for kids. When we uphold a boundary it tells kids that we are consistent and that they can count on us.

- **Meet them where they're at.** When you think of your relationships with different people, you likely act in different ways depending on who they are. You might go hiking with your friend who loves the outdoors or head to a quiet coffee shop with a friend who you can talk with for hours. Meeting kids where they are means that we actively learn what kids like, what's going on in their life, and bend toward them.

NAMING OUR BELIEFS AND ALIGNING OUR ACTIONS

While the beliefs and practices in this chapter are at the heart of this social-emotional work with children, they are also not an exhaustive list. You will also bring your own additional or different beliefs to this important work. It may be helpful to think about which parts of the beliefs you've read about in this book resonate with you, as well as which ones you would add. Naming our beliefs can help us get clear about our values and help us with another important step, ensuring our actions and practices align with our beliefs.

As teachers, we make an incredible number of decisions each day. Sometimes this can lead us to inevitably adopt practices or fall into routines without really examining the "why" behind them. I found myself noticing this one day when my class of kindergarteners was reciting our pre-going-into-the-hallway song, about having their hands by their side, standing straight and tall. The song was describing getting ready to walk in an almost-soldier-like line in the hallway, something I had grown to question and no longer aligned with my beliefs that kids are decision makers. I wanted my students to make choices about how their bodies walked down the hallway, teaching them multiple ways to be mindful of others. This awareness of misalignment helped me revise my practices and change course, choosing to co-create a class promise ("In the hallway we promise to be quiet, be safe, let other friends learn, and be kind to their work") for reminders of how to live into our values in the hallway.

As we continue this work throughout the rest of the book, it's helpful to have these beliefs and ones you've added close by. When we're observing children, responding to behaviors, and making decisions about what skills and strategies we might teach, we want to cross-check our actions with our beliefs to ensure we're living into them. Before moving on-to the next chapter, consider the following guiding questions on the next pages to reflect on bringing these beliefs into our practices. These questions may also be helpful to return to and discuss with a trusted colleague as you support one another in the ongoing work of reimagining classroom management and social-emotional learning.

BELIEF #1: THERE'S NO SUCH THING AS A BAD KID

- What might this child be trying to communicate?
- What might they need?
- What parts of the story am I missing?
- What do I not know about this child?

BELIEF #2: CHILDREN BRING BRILLIANCE TO SCHOOL

- What is this child interested in?
- Where are they most confident?
- Who are they drawn to?
- What do they see as their strengths?
- What can I learn from how their family knows them?
- What assumptions or biases might I have that could be affecting how I interact with this child? How can I disrupt these in order to have an asset-based view of this child?

BELIEF #3: KIDS ARE DECISION MAKERS

- Where can I provide opportunities for kids to try this new idea/routine/structure out?
- Where can I integrate more opportunities for kids to make decisions?
- How can I support kids in developing their decision-making skills?

BELIEF #4: COMMUNITY IS ESSENTIAL

- Where are the kids and their families represented in the classroom?
- Is this classroom set up in a way that is developmentally appropriate for the needs of my kids?
- Is there opportunity for movement and choice?
- Are materials accessible to kids? How do the kids interact with each other?

BELIEF #5: LANGUAGE IS ONE OF OUR MOST POWERFUL TOOLS

- How do I want kids to feel in our classroom?
- How do the kids want to feel in the classroom?
- What language and tone will convey this?
- Are there words/terms/language I want to stop using? What language will I use instead?

BELIEF #6: ROUTINES AND PREDICTABILITY CREATE A SENSE OF SAFETY

- What routines and procedures will I need to explicitly teach and why?
- How might I co-create these with children?
- How will I teach them?
- How will we practice them?

BELIEF #7: RELATIONSHIPS ARE CRITICAL FOR GROWTH

- How will I nurture relationships with my students?
- How will I help them nurture relationships with one another?

Chapter 3

The Process

Jocelyn was a fiery first grader who was always looking for opportunities to be in charge. She loved to hang around my table asking if there were any "jobs" or things I needed help with. She loved to be the boss, and when other kids would ask to join whatever she was doing, she reveled in the opportunity to decide who would be included and who would be pushed out. When she'd see a kid eagerly walking over to the sand table, she'd rush over to get there first, taking the last available seat. When playing "family" she always wanted to be the mom, commanding the others until they slunk away in frustration or ended up in tears. She dominated conversations, and if someone said something she didn't like, she was quick to give out a sharp insult, often resulting in her peer making a beeline for myself or another teacher to complain. Jocelyn's friendships were fragile.

One day after school, I was rearranging math partnerships and struggling with who to partner Jocelyn with. I often paired her with my most patient students, but had run through them and knew they likely needed a break. Yet I knew putting her with other strong-willed kids always ended up in fights. I resolved to pause my partnering and spend the next day simply observing Jocelyn, limiting my interventions and trying to stay as neutral as possible. On that day of observing, I spent a lot of time watching Jocelyn's facial expressions and body language. While Jocelyn's actions appeared confident and dominating, her facial expressions often seemed unsure and even worried.

That afternoon I read through my observations and reflected on the day. I noticed that while peer interactions were often contentious and strained with Joceyln, she kept attempting to engage with her peers. She was rarely chosen by her peers, and her interactions were more often argumentative than pleasant, but Jocelyn kept going back. Despite how difficult it must have been, a huge strength of Jocelyn's was her persistence. She clearly valued and desired relationships and peer interaction. Like all children (and adults), Jocelyn had a need for connection and belonging, even if the ways she sought it sometimes suggested the opposite. She just didn't yet have the skills to help her engage and meet that need of building relationships in a productive and healthy way.

That day my perspective on Jocelyn changed. I shifted from pigeon-holing Jocelyn into a "bossy" role, to having deep empathy for her. Jocelyn wasn't trying to be problematic. She wasn't hoping to push her friends away. Jocelyn was using the skills she currently had to attempt to meet a need for peer relationships. This new perspective propelled me to plan out ways to teach Jocelyn how to build and maintain friendships, helping her to meet that need and develop the social and emotional skills that would help her (and her classmates) flourish.

INTRODUCING THE PROCESS

My first few years teaching, I was often perplexed by why some students just wouldn't "follow the rules." I felt confident that the kids knew what the expectations were, but was unsure about what was getting in the way of them meeting those expectations. Was I not clear enough? Were some students just choosing not to follow the expectations? Luckily, around the same time, I was fortunate enough to discover Ross Greene's book, *Lost at School,* which provided an alternative idea for what might be going on. Greene writes, "in the case of challenging kids, it's not that they don't know how we want them to behave, it's that they're lacking the skills to execute what they know" (2014, 39).

As I read more of Greene's work, my mindset around children's behavior started to shift. I thought about our process for teaching academic skills—assess, plan, teach, reflect—and how I view both the children's role and my own role in that learning process. When I think about teaching academic skills, like teaching letter names to kindergarteners, I would never assume a child knows I want them to learn the names of the letters but they're just choosing not to learn them. Instead, I would assess what they currently can do, plan responsive instruction, break down the skill to manageable parts, and reflect on how my teaching is having an impact. I'd work with them to develop the skills they need to meet the expectations. So, why is it different with behavior?

In this chapter, we'll explore an alternative approach to teaching and supporting students' social and emotional learning. This process emerged from my own frustration of knowing that often what we were doing for kids with regards to responding to behavior not only wasn't working, it also wasn't equitable. We'll go beyond the idea that student behavior is an issue to be "fixed" and instead explore ways we can support students' individual and group needs in ways that foster a strong classroom community. When we notice students struggling to demonstrate the social-emotional skills they need to thrive, we'll engage in a process (Figure 3.1) to support them in developing those skills. In subsequent chapters, we'll also explore common social-emotional ideas related to behaviors. Each idea will have its own chapter with accompanying lessons that utilize these same teaching methods and processes. So, let's jump in!

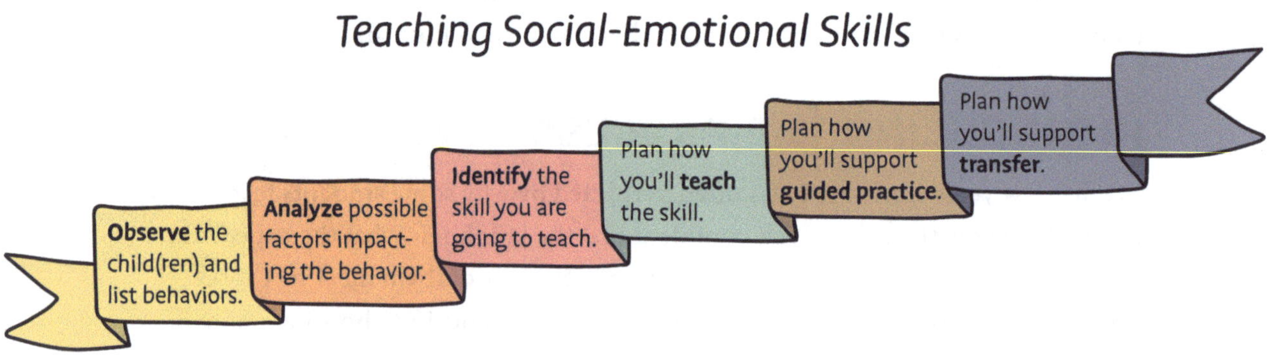

Figure 3.1 *A process for analyzing and teaching social-emotional skills.*

STEP 1: OBSERVE AND CHOOSE A FOCUS

The first step in the process is to slow down and give yourself permission to take the time to observe a child, group of children, or class. In the constant state of do-more-with-less in education, there , can be a frantic pressure to just keep pressing on. But there is so much to learn when we pause and observe. When I paused to observe and reflect on Jocelyn, I shifted from managing her behavior to understanding it and teaching her the skills she needed to be successful.

When we get into problem-solving mode it's easy to focus our attention on the maladaptive behaviors. The hitting, the eloping, the yelling can, at times, feel like all we can see. And yet, each child has a multitude of skills and strengths that are also helpful for us to notice and which provide further insight into the child as a full person. When observing through this lens, it can be hard not to fall into this dichotomy mindset of looking for and labeling "good" and "bad" behaviors. In this process, however, we'll take an alternative approach, focusing less on the labeling of the behaviors and more on understanding what's behind them. If you are someone who finds it helpful to organize behaviors *and* want to maintain a child-centered perspective, you might consider using the table with guiding headings in Figure 3.2.

Teaching Social-Emotional Skills Form	
Step 1: Observe	
Behaviors that the child is successful with or serve them in a healthy way	Behaviors that the child is struggling with or that serve them in a maladaptive way

Figure 3.2 *The first step of the Teaching Social-Emotional Skills Form is observing.*

Before you jump into recording your observations, a quick note about the content of what we write down. When I first started writing down observations, I would write things like "great friend" or "can't sit still." And while at times it can feel efficient to synthesize behaviors in this way, we can end up with labels that feel subjective and carry judgment. These kinds of observations can also make it harder to see the specific skills that are within those labels. What makes them a great friend? Do they include others, take turns, problem-solve effectively? The more specific we can be, the better. What parts about sitting-still are hard? Body awareness? Distractions? Self-regulation? Figure 3.3 has examples of how we might shift from more subjective, broader terms to more specific observations.

After you've had time to record your observations, you'll want to read through and see what you're noticing. What behaviors and skills does the child currently have success with? What behaviors indicate the child is having a hard time? You'll narrow your focus on one area. This focus might come from a skill that you're noticing is a strength of the child's (i.e., making friends) and you want to build on that (i.e., how to speak up when you want to do something different than your friend). Another likely area to focus on is where you notice the child struggling. I'll often read through the list of observations and see which behaviors seem to be having the biggest

More Subjective Label	More Objective Observation
Kind	Includes others by asking them if they want to play
Mean	Has a hard time making friends and navigating disagreements with peers
Defiant	Has a hard time coping with being asked to engage in non-preferred tasks

Figure 3.3 *Avoiding subjective labels and attempting to more objectively describe observations helps us more clearly understand children.*

impact on the child and the community around them. I tend to prioritize behaviors that are impacting the physical or emotional safety of the child or their peers first as they often feel more urgent to tackle. For example, if a child is both eloping and not engaging in their work, I would prioritize teaching skills and strategies to meet the need of safety in the classroom before tackling work completion.

Figure 3.4 *A teacher observes a group of students to see how they navigate sharing a new game that many students want to play.*

STEP 2: ANALYZE AND DIG DEEPER

Once you've picked a focus, the next step in analyzing and teaching social-emotional skills is to dig a little deeper to see what might be impacting and influencing a behavior. Spend a little more time observing with that behavior in mind. There really is power in pausing and watching kids. I remember saying to a colleague that one of my students was "constantly interrupting and talking to others." We decided to observe him the following day and realized that the behavior really only happened during independent work time and, upon listening in on exactly what he was saying to his classmates, he was sharing on-topic comments about what he was reading or working on. Was this still distracting to the class? Yes. Would I still need to teach him about the impact of interrupting on others and strategies to navigate conversations? Yes. But it helped me move past a generalized judgment of a student being disruptive to a more specific skill to teach him. It also helped shift my perception of the student. The child wasn't trying to intentionally disrupt the class (which was slowly becoming the internal narrative in my head), but instead was so enthusiastic about his learning that he wanted to share it with others.

BEHAVIOR IS COMMUNICATION

Behaviors are often outward expressions of how a child is trying to get a need met. In their book *Relationships, Responsibility and Regulation: Trauma-Invested Practices for Fostering Resilient Learners,* authors Souers and Hall write about the importance of understanding the needs underneath behavior, writing, "often in education, we get bogged down in *how* a student is trying to get a need met instead of focusing on what the student's need *is*" (2019, 52). Typically children's needs fall into one of these categories: emotional need, relational need, physical need, or control need (Souers and Hall 2018). Kids are trying their best to meet their needs with the skills they currently have. My student, Jocelyn, from the opening story of this chapter, likely had an unmet relational need. She was yearning to feel connected to others and, despite her behaviors on the surface, had a deep desire to feel loved and included. Disciplining or reprimanding Jocelyn for her behaviors likely would not have influenced a meaningful change but would certainly have risked making her feel more isolated. She might have adapted her behaviors, but the unmet need would still remain.

Here are some questions to consider when observing students:

- When does the behavior occur? When does it not occur?
- Where does the behavior occur? Where does it not occur?

- Who is the child around when the behavior occurs?
- What happens right before the behavior occurs? What happens right after the behavior occurs?
- What needs might the child be trying to communicate through their behavior?
- Is this behavior important for us to focus on? Why?

STEP 3: IDENTIFY THE SKILL

Now that you have analyzed your observations and decided on a focus, the next step is to think about what skill to teach. It's important to keep in mind what our purpose is when teaching kids skills. Are we teaching skills to encourage compliance or are we teaching skills that are relevant and helpful to kids in school *and* in different parts of their lives? Remember, we're working to bring awareness to what behaviors and skills are traditionally (and problematically) idealized in schools and working to avoid trying to get kids to conform to these norms at the risk of harm to themselves and their identities. One strategy to help ensure the skill is meaningful to kids is to probe for the rationale behind the skill. Why do we ask kids to sit crisscross? For me, it was so that all kids could see and have space. If that's our rationale, we want to first teach kids why we need to be aware of our bodies in the group meeting space, and second teach them the *many* ways they can ensure all kids can see and have space (i.e., look behind you to make sure the person can see, sit in the back row if you want to be on your knees). A helpful check is to see if we're providing kids with multiple ways to utilize a skill. Oftentimes more compliance-based skills have one "right" way, whereas more community-focused skills have an adaptable repertoire of choices, giving the child more autonomy and the ability to cross-check their decisions with the community-focused rationale. Figure 3.5 illustrates some examples of the nuanced differences with this.

Sometimes the social-emotional skills to teach jump out to us right away, while other times it can feel challenging to think about what skill might help a kid be successful. Remember that you aren't ruining a child by teaching "the wrong skill" first. What's important is that we're closely observing and responding specifically to the children in front of us. There have been times where I tried to teach a skill to a child and then realized there was another skill that I needed to back up and teach them first. We try something, see how it goes, and revise as needed. This isn't a checklist to complete, but rather a journey of building up skills

Observation	Compliance-Focused Skill (Often more conventional "school" skills)	Community-Focused Skill
Shouting out	How to always raise your hand to speak	Some ways to listen for an opening in the conversation to speak
Refusal to give up toys	When someone asks for a toy, you always share it	Some ways to respond when someone asks you for something
Talking in the hallway	How to walk in a straight, silent line with your hands by your side.	Some ways to be mindful of others when walking in the hallway

Figure 3.5 *Identifying a community-focused skill rather than a compliance-focused one is a meaningful part of reimagining classroom management and social-emotional learning.*

for kids' social and emotional growth. Most importantly, we honor children's strengths and challenges and teach in ways that honor their agency and value as community members. Figure 3.6 shows some examples of observations and what skill could be a good fit.

Observation	Social-Emotional Skill to Teach
Difficulty coping with mistakes	Some ways to choose a strategy when you make a mistake
Difficulty managing emotions	Some ways to pick a coping skill and a safe space
Difficulty sharing	Some ways to share and respond when you're not ready to share
Difficulty maintaining friendships	Some ways to work through problems that arise with your friends

Figure 3.6 *Our careful observations of children's strengths and challenges can help us choose a skill to teach.*

BEING MINDFUL OF ALL THAT GOES INTO A SKILL

Sometimes deciding on what skill to teach seems obvious. A student is dysregulated and eloping from the classroom? Teach them how to regulate and stay in the classroom. And for some kids that works and they take on the skill right away. For many others though, they need us to break down the skill into more manageable chunks. In those moments I often think of a staircase image (Figure 3.7) that illustrates the process of breaking down both academic and social-emotional instruction into smaller parts. In this scenario eloping would be on the bottom step and using a regulation strategy in the classroom would be on the top. So, what would be the in-between steps? Perhaps the child first needs to be taught how to notice when they're dysregulated so that they can *then* identify a strategy to use. Or maybe it's utilizing a current coping strategy (like leaving the classroom) in a safer way to show trust in the child and their body signaling to them to flee. It's important to remember that we work within a child's zone of proximal development both with academics and social-emotional skills. So, if a child is showing us that they're

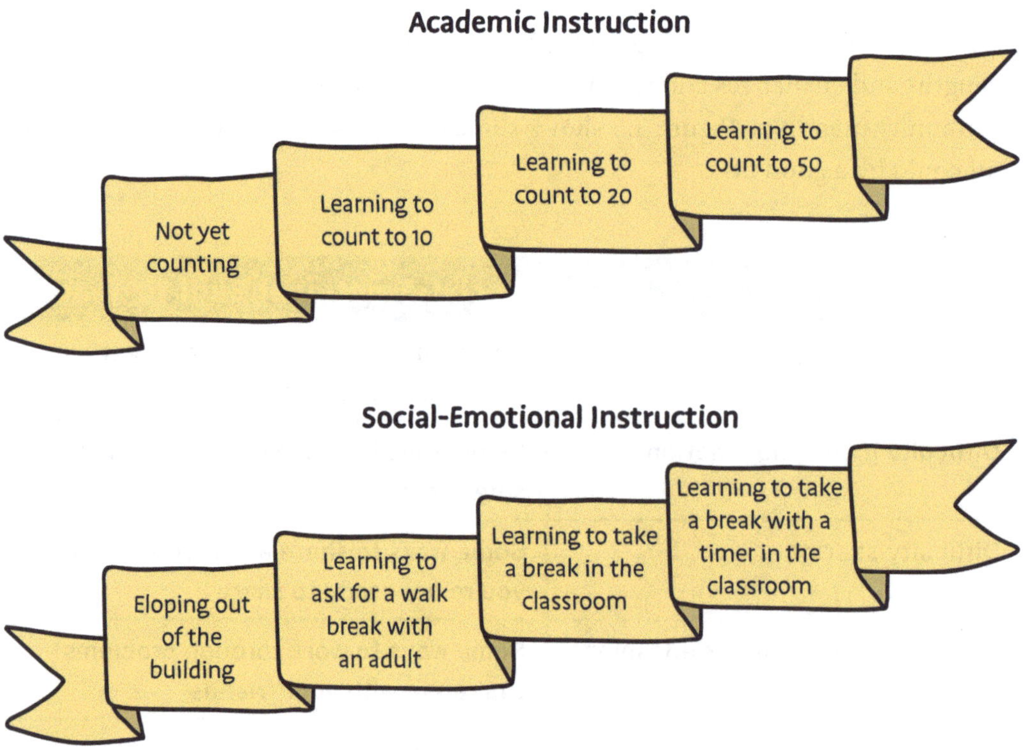

Figure 3.7 *A comparison of how to break down academic and social-emotional instruction into smaller parts using a staircase model.*

dysregulated and grasping for control by eloping, we're not going to keep telling them to *just sit in their seat,* just as I wouldn't tell a child who was just starting to count that they *just needed to count to 100.*

STEP 4: PLAN FOR HOW YOU'LL TEACH THE SKILL

In this next step we'll get into the nitty gritty of teaching a social-emotional skill. When we teach academic content, we use a variety of methods. In math, I might introduce a concept through a number talk, a math task, a whole-class conversation, or a math game. We choose different methods depending on our purpose and often end up using a combination of methods to thoroughly teach and give practice with a new skill. Similarly, there are a variety of teaching methods we can utilize to teach students social and emotional skills. All of these methods can be utilized with a class, small group, or individual students.

TEACHING METHOD: CLASS CONVERSATION AND CONFERENCES

A class conversation provides an opportunity for all students to be involved in a discussion about either a problem to solve or a skill you want to bring into focus. These conversations might look like the teacher sharing something they've been noticing going on and asking for feedback and ideas for how to address it. It might sound like, "I've been noticing recently that when we're playing soccer during recess that some of us are trying to solve our problems using our bodies. Soccer is important to us and I want us to work together to figure out another way to solve our problems in a safe way when we're feeling upset." It's helpful to record proposed solutions on an anchor chart as an artifact of the conversation we can refer back to. A class conversation is a helpful choice when your observations show you that many students in the class would benefit from learning a specific skill. It can also be helpful in giving the whole class language and understanding around a skill. So even if it's only a few kids fighting on the soccer field, you've now equipped all of the students with language and strategies to help each other.

Conferences can follow a similar structure as class conversations, but with individuals or a smaller group of students. We can present the problem in a similar way, "I'm noticing ____" and then work together with the student(s) to gather more information and decide what skills we can build to support them.

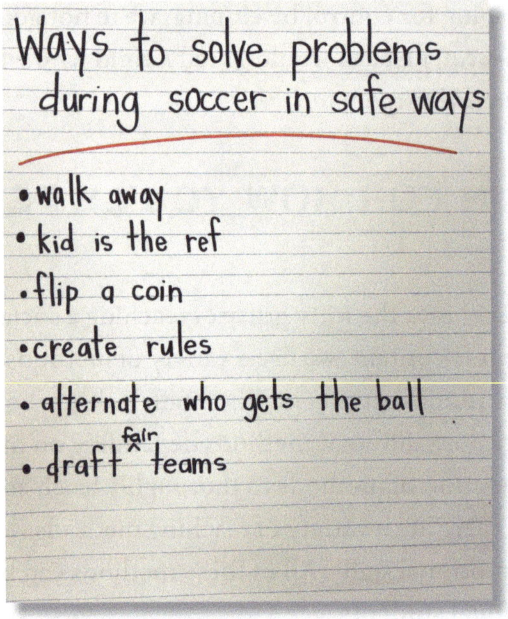

Figure 3.8 *Chart with student-generated suggestions for a class problem.*

Figure 3.9 *Mari guides a class conversation about friendship in which the students share and write their ideas on a chart.*

TEACHING METHOD: EXPLICIT INSTRUCTION WITH STEPS OR STRATEGIES

With this teaching method we explicitly teach students the steps or strategies for a skill that we've observed the students would benefit from. While class conversations tend to be more collaborative and inquiry based, explicit instruction is more of a "today I'm going to teach you" style of delivery. While explicit, this instruction is still invitational and encourages students to find additional strategies of their own. It might sound like, "We've been learning about ways to respond when someone does something that makes us angry. Today I'm going to teach you one strategy you might try, which is to walk away and take some breaths." This teaching method is a helpful one to utilize when you haven't seen many students using the skill yet or you have specific strategies you think would be beneficial for them to try. You can always open up the discussion for feedback or other ideas after launching with a more explicit start. This might sound like, "What other strategies for regulating do you like to use when you're angry?"

Figure 3.10 *Mari points to a strategy chart.*

STEP 5: PLAN FOR GUIDED PRACTICE

The next step in this process for analyzing and teaching social-emotional skills is all about guided practice. Have you ever taught a focus lesson and thought to yourself, "wow, I really nailed that." Yet, later when you looked at students' work, there was minimal evidence of them taking on the new learning? I certainly have found myself in this situation a number of times. Sometimes we forget, or don't spend enough time on, the important step of guided practice. We jump from "I do" to "you do" and forget the essential "we do" part in the middle. It would be as if my horseback riding instructor were to give me a lesson on how to canter for the first time and then released me into the field, alone, to try it all by myself. It wouldn't end well! The guided practice part of a lesson is essential to helping new learning stick. This is our opportunity to help students take on the skill independently. If you've ever felt like "they know what to do, but they're just not doing it," this is the place to focus. The three main teaching methods we'll focus on are role play and scenarios, social stories, and interactive read-aloud.

TEACHING METHOD: ROLE PLAY AND SCENARIOS

Role play is a strategy where students get to practice using a skill by acting out a situation. It's a helpful method to use especially when you notice students are able to articulate what using a specific skill would look like, but aren't yet putting it into practice yet. This might look like asking two volunteer students to sit in the middle of the carpet with a high-interest toy and asking them to try out one of the strategies they've been learning about sharing, while the rest of the class sits on the outside of the carpet ready to support and reflect.

While some kids love the stage during a role play, others might not (especially in the upper elementary grades). Similar goals can be accomplished by talking through scenarios. With a scenario, you can verbally pose a situation or put up an image (e.g., two kids in the lunchroom pushing each other to sit on the same seat) and ask kids to talk through what they're noticing and what strategies they would use to navigate the situation. This is a great way to practice and capture the language kids use when trying out strategies. As adults, we might say "can I have that when you're done?" when trying out turn taking, but to kids, "me next, bruh?" might be how they do it.

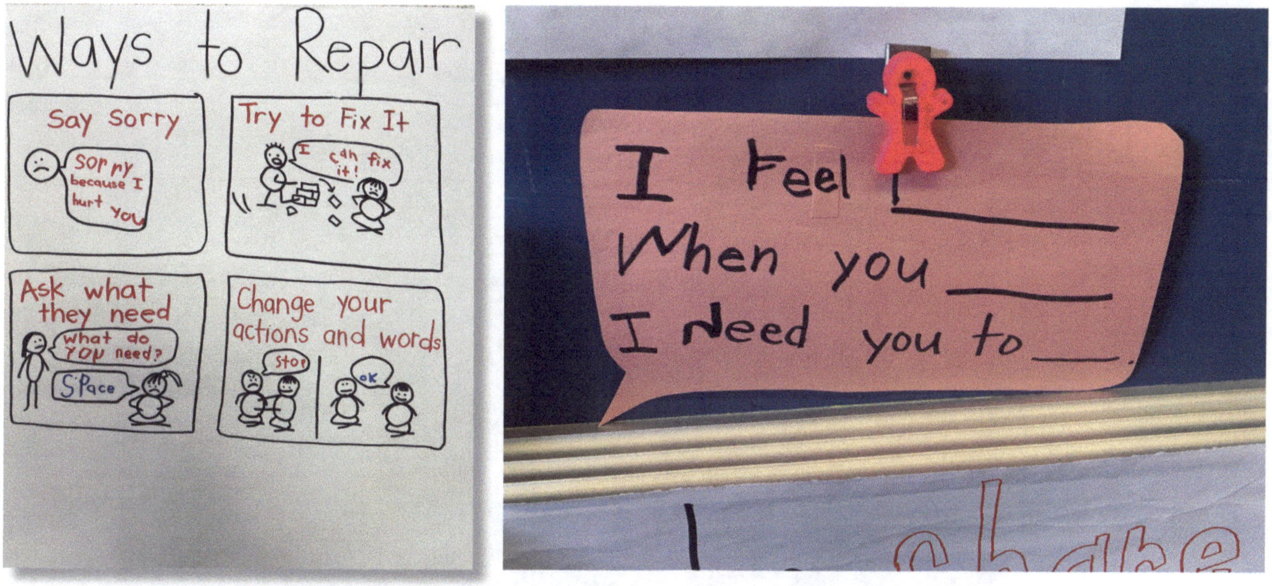

Figure 3.11 *A chart with sample language generated by kids (left) and some sample language on a small chart for students to use when problem solving together (right).*

Talking through scenarios together helps kids build and internalize the skill in a way that feels meaningful and realistic to them. It can be helpful to capture some of the language kids use as sentence stems on charts.

So where can we get ideas for all these role-play scenarios? The kids! Observe kids with the skill you're trying to teach in mind. What moments are bubbling up in the classroom that show kids could use some skill practice through role play? One year I had a group of kindergarteners who would get into heated arguments that led to lots of dysregulation and unkind things being said. After observing, I realized they needed to learn about how to have a productive argument and how to get out of an argument you don't want to be in. Together as a class we talked about some different strategies and got ready to role play. I wrote down scenarios like, "What would you do if someone said sharks are the best animal but you don't think they are?" They easily role-played a calm discussion about favorite animals. Then, as we transitioned to the carpet for our read-aloud, a fierce argument erupted over who got to the carpet "first." I realized then that this was the scenario we actually needed to practice. It can be helpful to jot down a bank of scenarios as moments occur to utilize when you're practicing.

Figure 3.12 *Two students sit facing each other role playing a scenario. The other students sit in a circle around them watching, ready to reflect together afterward.*

TEACHING METHOD: SOCIAL STORIES

Social stories were developed by Carol Gray, a teacher who specializes in supporting children with autism, as a tool to support children with anticipating what to expect and what strategies they might utilize in a certain situation. Social stories are short texts you can create yourself that provide a comfortable, predictable story that can be read over and over. They are a great tool for supporting kids with internalizing a skill. When writing social stories for kids I typically follow a sequential structure. Figures 3.13 and 3.14 show examples of social stories.

Playing Games with My Friends

Sometimes when I play games I win. Sometimes I don't win.

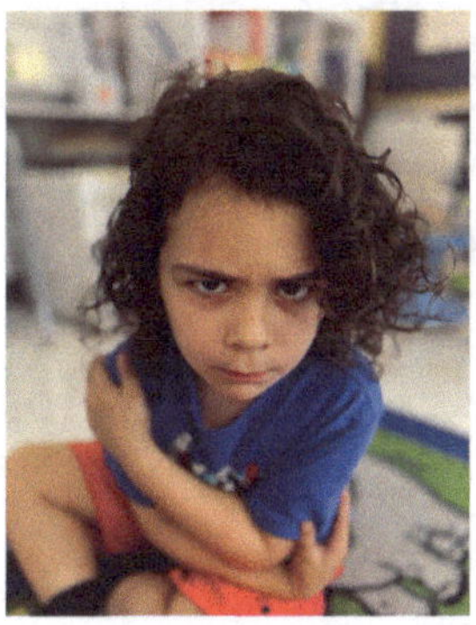

When I don't win, I might feel mad.

When I feel mad, I can take a deep breath and use my tools.

When I feel better, I can go back and play again!

Figure 3.13 *An example of a social story created for a student using photographs.*

Figure 3.14 *An example of a social story collaboratively created with the class and illustrated by the students.*

Similar to how making role-play scenarios "realer" for kids by pulling from their own experiences, photographs of the child can help make the story feel more relatable and meaningful.

TEACHING METHOD: INTERACTIVE READ-ALOUDS

Interactive read-alouds are opportunities to read a text aloud to children while utilizing intentional stopping points throughout the text and at the end for discussion. When using this teaching method, gather texts that either explicitly or implicitly address the skill you are trying to teach. For example, if you're teaching about how to be a good friend you might choose books that are explicitly giving

Figure 3.15 *Mari reads aloud a book and poses questions for the children to discuss together.*

ideas for how to be a good friend. You might also choose books that include relatable opportunities for kids to apply the skill to the characters. For example, you might read a text where a kid's friend is being teased in order to foster a discussion around being a good friend in tricky situations. You can strategically plan a stopping point at that part of the book and prompt a discussion. You might ask the group, "What would you do if you were that friend?" or "What strategy might the character try?" Interactive read-alouds are a helpful choice especially when you notice kids feeling resistant to taking on a skill on their own. There's something about the distance characters have from us that can make us feel safer when discussing and trying out new skills and strategies.

Figure 3.16 *Mari sits beside a student and coaches them to pick a strategy to help them work through making a mistake.*

STEP 6: PLAN TO SUPPORT TRANSFER

The final step in this process for analyzing and teaching social-emotional skills focuses on supporting transfer. We've done some explicit teaching (I do), some guided practice together (we do), and now kids are trying it out on their own (you do). In an effort to support this "you do" transfer we can utilize strategies such as pre-conferences, coaching, timeouts, and reflections to help set kids up for success.

TEACHING METHOD: PRE-CONFERENCES

Pre-conferences are an opportunity to visualize an upcoming situation and think through helpful responses. Kennedy describes this as building up our children's "emotion regulation antibodies" as a way to pre-regulate (2022, 128). Think about moments throughout the day that are ripe with opportunities for a child to try out the skill you're teaching them. If you're working on how to cope with losing a game, consider a pre-conference with the class to talk through possible strategies they can use before playing a class game. If lunch seems to be a particularly hard time for students to stay regulated, have a quick pre-conference before heading to the cafeteria about what issues might crop up and how the kids can respond. This might sound like,

> The last ten minutes of lunch have been an extra tricky time for us to stay regulated. What are some strategies you might use if you finish your lunch early and notice your body getting dysregulated? How might you help your friends with this?

TEACHING METHOD: COACHING

Coaching is in-the-moment teaching, prompting, and reinforcing. Similar to what we do when we teach academics, when we coach we are giving kids feedback in the moment when they're trying something out. Just as my riding instructor will be in my ear before a jump to remind me of technique or praise my efforts as I land, we can do the same thing with kids when they're trying out new skills. To do this, we need to be up and in close proximity to kids. This might look like hanging close by a student who's learning to persist through challenges when they're working through a difficult task. It might sound like,

> I notice your body is getting tense as you're working on that drawing. Let's check in with your body and see what strategy you might try to help you keep going and feeling good.

Remember, language is one of our most powerful tools!

TEACHING METHOD: TIMEOUTS

These aren't the sit-in-a-chair-and-face-the-wall kind of timeouts, but rather the timeouts a coach calls during a sports game. These timeouts are helpful in-the-moment pauses where the class can work together to think through using a new skill.

This might look like noticing that kids keep distracting each other during work time. It could sound like,

> Let's take a quick time out. I'm noticing lots of distractions bubbling up today while friends are trying to work independently. Let's remind ourselves, what are some things we can say or do when someone comes up to us when we're trying to focus on our work?

Have a few kids share out and/or reference the strategy chart and then get right back to learning, giving kids the immediate opportunity to apply those skills.

TEACHING METHOD: REFLECTIONS

Reflections serve as an opportunity to look back and reflect on how a situation went with the lens of the skill students are learning. Reflection conversations can be helpful to have after a moment in which a child tried (or did not try) a strategy. You might use a reflection to celebrate the use of a strategy. Or maybe a strategy wasn't used and you want to talk through a do-over. For a class that is learning how to include others, it might sound like,

> We've been learning how to include others, and today I saw Kate use a strategy at recess–asking someone if they want to join her–when she saw someone sitting alone. Kate, how did that go? What did you notice about how you were feeling? How about the other friend?

If a strategy or situation doesn't go as planned and a student is dysregulated or escalated, it can be helpful to wait until they are regulated and feel ready to reflect on the situation. This might sound like, "I know it was really tough when you were trying to be persistent with the paint and then the water spilled. Do you feel ready to talk about it or do you want more time?"

PUTTING IT ALL TOGETHER

Now that we've learned a process for teaching social-emotional skills as well as some different methods for doing this kind of teaching, let's take a look at the parts of this process in action with both a class and individual student.

TEACHING SOCIAL-EMOTIONAL SKILLS: CLASS EXAMPLE

Snapshot: *It's writing workshop time and despite the soothing classical music playing in the background, it's anything but calm in here. Ashley walks up to me distraught claiming, "Grace is sitting in MY spot!" Before I can even begin to coach Ashley in problem solving, Bryan runs up with tears in his eyes yelling, "Jhonny just wrote on my paper!!!" Jhonny is interestingly avoiding all eye contact when I look over to confirm the recounting of these events. As I'm asking Bryan to wait for a moment so I can support Ashley, I look out and see Ghita and Joshua moments away from a brawl over a green marker. As they catch my eye, they both run up to me ready to plead their cases and hope that I rule in their favor.*

Teaching Social-Emotional Skills Form	
Step 1: Observe	
Behaviors that the child is successful with or serve them in a healthy way	Behaviors that the child is struggling with or that serve them in a maladaptive way
• Confidence speaking up when they think an injustice has occurred • Ability to articulate what is concerning them	• Having a hard time talking directly to the person they have a problem with • Having a hard time navigating sharing • Unsure about boundaries related to personal space (seats, papers, etc.)
Step 2: Analyze and Dig Deeper	
• I notice that kids tend to come up to me more to solve problems during less structured times (play, recess, independent work time). It seems to occur more when there are limited quantities of something, making sharing necessary (exp. only a few toy cars). • I'm wondering if one of the unmet needs of the class is related to boundaries and safety related to space and resources. Are there ample spaces and resources available to kids? • I'm wondering what is motivating the kids to come to teachers instead of their peers. Do they believe they can solve problems on their own? Are their peers not listening unless an adult gets involved?	

While all of these behaviors would be helpful to address and teach the class, the most pressing one right now is that kids aren't talking directly to the person they have a problem with. Once they start doing this, I'll be able to gather more information on what they need additional support with (asking for what they need, ways to share, etc.)

Step 3: Identify a Skill

How to talk directly to the person you need to problem solve with

Step 4: Plan for How You'll Teach the Skill

One way we might teach this is...

Explicit Instruction with Steps or Strategies

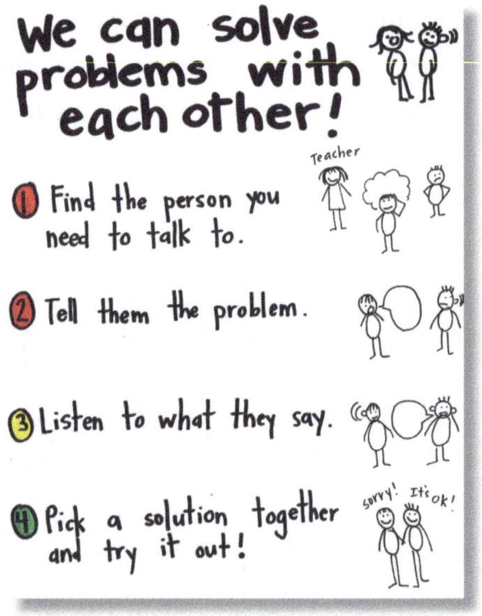

Figure 3.17 *We Can Solve Problems with Each Other Chart.*

Step 5: Plan for Guided Practice

One way we might practice this is...

Role Play/Scenario

As a class, we'll practice some of the scenarios that have been happening recently. For example, I'll choose two students to volunteer and act out this scenario: *Angel colored on Bridget's paper and Bridget was really upset. Let's watch who she goes to talk to in this first step!* Point to chart (3.17). I'll highlight that she didn't go to the teacher or to her friend, she went right to Angel. We'll work through the rest of the scenario, reflecting on the various parts together.

Step 6: Plan for Transfer

One way we might support transfer is...

Coaching

This part is twofold. First, I'm going to have to coach myself and perhaps pick a mantra to say to myself when the kids come to me to solve their problems (i.e., "I want to empower kids to solve their own problems."). This can help me avoid the trap of putting out fires which unintentionally robs kids of the opportunity to utilize their problem-solving skills with each other. Second, I want to help the kids feel successful with this. When problems start to arise, I'll slip my voice in or slide them a smaller version of the chart we all created together (Figure 3.17) to scaffold the important work that the kids are doing as they try this out on their own. I'll keep my coaching language focused on generative steps the kids can take (i.e., "What's a strategy you could pick?" instead of "Tell her you're sorry").

Figure 3.18 *An example of a Teaching Social-Emotional Skills Form for a whole-class focus.*

TEACHING SOCIAL-EMOTIONAL SKILLS: INDIVIDUAL KID EXAMPLE

Snapshot: *It's a rainy day and we're having indoor recess. Alexander is attempting to draw a great white shark and I can tell by his increasingly tense body and frustrated sounds that it's not going the way he envisioned. As I start to walk closer to support him, I realize I'm too late as he rips the paper and kicks over his chair. After a short break, Alexander appears regulated and I see him go back to get a new piece of paper. I'm already tense myself as this has been an increasing pattern of behavior when Alexander perceives he's made a mistake. I see him start to draw the shark's head and when it doesn't go the way he wants he flails his arms, sending the bin of markers and pens flying across the room.*

Teaching Social-Emotional Skills Form	
Step 1: Observe	
Behaviors that the child is successful with or serve them in a healthy way	**Behaviors that the child is struggling with or that serve them in a maladaptive way**
• Determined to complete challenging tasks • Often says kind words to others about their work and style	• Quickly getting dysregulated when making a mistake (throwing/ripping things) • Unsure how to work through making a mistake • Perfectionist pressure on self

All of these skills are important to address and some will likely take more time than others. I envision shifting to a more malleable, growth mindset about mistakes as a long game goal. Something that we'll work on through read-alouds, discussions, and lots of coaching. The most pressing skill right now is to help the child get regulated enough to make a decision about how to safely work through mistakes.

Step 2: Analyze and Dig Deeper

- I notice that Alexander seems to work through making a "mistake" when building with Magna-Tiles or Legos much easier than with drawing and writing. This makes me wonder if there's something about the "permanence" of mistakes for him since he gets the most upset with mistakes when he's drawing or writing on paper
- I notice the behavior occurs with or without teacher support present. Strategies like drawing an example for Alexander or using a model to copy only increase his frustration, making me wonder if he thinks that his drawings need to be "as good" as "the real thing."
- I'm wondering if he has an unmet emotional need, the need to be able to regulate himself in times of distress.

Step 3: Identify a Skill

How to help myself when I feel a BIG feeling

At first I was going to teach "How to use a strategy when we make a mistake," but when I thought about the staircase visual (Figure 3.7), I realized Alexander likely first needs to get himself regulated enough to choose a strategy.

Step 4: Plan for How You'll Teach the Skill

One way we might teach this is...

Explicit Instruction with Steps or Strategies

Figure 3.19 *When I Have a Big Feeling I Can... Chart.*

Step 5: Plan for Guided Practice
One way we might practice this is...

Role Play

When Alexander is regulated, we'll practice talking through some scenarios (using a mix of ones I've already witnessed and ones that I anticipate could lead to him becoming dysregulated). I'll encourage Alexander to pick a strategy (Figure 3.19) and practice using it.

Step 6: Plan for Transfer
One way we might support transfer is...

Pre-Conference

Before Alexander engages in something that I anticipate might lead to big feelings, we'll talk through which strategies he might use. I'll prepare him as much as possible (have the chart and any supportive tools nearby to easily and nonverbally reference).

Figure 3.20 *An example of a Teaching Social-Emotional Skills Form for an individual focus.*

As you get started with this work, it may be helpful to work with a colleague to think through and fill out the Teaching Social-Emotional Skills form, a blank version of which is in Figure 3.21 and in Appendix A.

Teaching Social Emotions Skills Form	
Step 1: Observe	
Behaviors that the child is successful with or serve them in a healthy way	Behaviors that the child is struggling with or that are serving them in a maladaptive way
Step 2: Analyze and Dig Deeper	
Step 3: Identify a Skill	
Step 4: Plan for How You'll Teach the Skill *One way we might teach this is...*	
Step 5: Plan for Guided Practice *One way we might practice this is...*	
Step 6: Plan for Transfer *One way we might support transfer is...*	

Figure 3.21 *The Teaching Social-Emotional Skills Form template.*

MOVING FORWARD

Now that we've explored different ways to observe and analyze behavior, identify needed skills, and various methods for teaching social-emotional skills, we're going to see this in action in the chapters that come. While there will be many sample lessons, remember that this process is a generative one that you can use to create your own responsive lessons at any time. As we do this work to reframe teaching social-emotional skills away from "fixing students" or "fixing problems" and toward a lens of helping kids grow their social-emotional skills, we can actually enjoy this process and celebrate kids' journeys and growth.

Chapter 4

Prelude to the Lessons

A few years ago, I was a part of a team reviewing the comprehensive needs of our school and impacting factors. After analyzing data and correlations, we concluded that "behavior" was one of the biggest factors impacting student learning. We started to unpack what we meant by "behavior" and what might be influencing the current state of student behavior in the school (for this exercise we focused on factors within our control). We then crafted actionable steps for the next few years to support teachers and staff in a way that could create powerful changes for our kids. In an effort to create common and shared beliefs about behavior we engaged in a book study of Carla Shalaby's book *Troublemakers: Lessons in Freedom from Young Children at School.*

After months of engaging in reading and dialogue about *Troublemakers,* we were lucky enough to have Carla speak to the staff in a culminating event. She was incredible. She pushed us to consider what she calls the "loving way," an approach in which we shift away from policing children and toward teaching kids skills and nudged us to view kids as decision makers who can learn to be mindful of themselves and others. Afterward as staff were talking a colleague shared, "I believe in this, but *how* do we actually teach it." There were so many emphatic nods by surrounding teachers. The question and response from colleagues revealed both evidence that we had grown in our alignment of beliefs *and* that we were ready for the essential next step—equipping teachers with the bridge to turn beliefs into practices. My colleague Jess turned to me and whispered, "this is why you have to write your book." And thus, the lessons section of this book emerged.

WHAT IS A STRATEGY LESSON?

This second section of this book is divided into four parts: Regulation (Chapter 5), Relationships (Chapter 6), Problem Solving (Chapter 7), and Agency (Chapter 8). Each chapter focuses on a big idea and the underlying skills that support that big idea. While there are many social-emotional skills and strategies I could have chosen to focus on within each of these chapters, I've selected the ones that students in Grades K-6 often need support and guidance to develop and the ones that will hopefully continue to serve them long after they leave elementary school. It's important to note that there are many other needs like freedom, power, and control that are woven throughout all of this work.

Within each skill chapter are strategy lessons. Jennifer Serravallo, author of *The Reading Strategies Book* and *The Writing Strategies Book,* who has written countless literacy strategy lessons, defines the purpose of strategies as making the invisible work visible (2015). The strategies in *Lessons in Community* aim to do just that by making typically abstract concepts like "be a good friend" or "pay attention" more concrete and actionable for kids. There are *many* strategies that can support individuals in developing a skill. The lessons in this book are far from an exhaustive list and my hope is that they are useful to you while also inspiring you to generate your own lessons to meet the needs of your kids.

One thing these lessons all have in common is that they take the stance that children already have skills and competencies they will bring to these lessons, and that we can draw on these skills and competencies in the classroom to help children continue to learn and grow. These lessons and our view of children are asset-based.

WHERE DO I START WITH THE STRATEGY LESSONS?

This book is set up in a way to support teachers with finding lessons that meet the unique needs of the students in front of them. This is one place where this book differs from typical social-emotional boxed curriculums in which every class starts at the same beginning and progresses in the same sequence. This kind of lock-step sequencing is where many teachers' frustration arises. If our kids are struggling with problem solving in September, but that lesson isn't scheduled until March, it's going to be a long year! This book is instead set up in a way that allows you to move flexibly between lessons and chapters depending on what you're noticing your individual kids need.

So where do you flip to first? Think back to "The Process" (Chapter 3) where we noticed children's social-emotional strengths and challenges and then chose a focus for what we might teach them next. Toward the end of each chapter, before the lessons, you'll find an "If You Notice ... You Might Try..." table. The "If You Notice" column of the table outlines some of the behaviors we, as teachers, might observe. The "You Might Try" column lists some possible strategy lessons we might teach to support children in developing helpful strategies. Lesson topics with numbers are strategies that have full lessons within the chapter, while lesson topics without numbers are there to spark ideas for other lessons you might create.

WHAT'S INSIDE EACH LESSON?

If we want kids to really take on new learning, we need to embed ample opportunities for practice and transfer with support. With this rationale in mind, each lesson has three main components for teaching: how we might *teach the strategy*, *practice the strategy*, and *support students with transfer*. The sample lessons illustrate *one way* you might teach the strategies, but I encourage you to innovate and adapt in ways that are responsive to the children in front of you. As you become familiar with the various teaching methods within these lessons, reflect on which ones match your purpose and use them flexibly.

ONE WAY WE MIGHT TEACH THIS

As noted in "The Process" (Chapter 3), there are many different teaching methods you could choose to teach a lesson. The *One Way We Might Teach This* section of each lesson provides one example method and sample teacher language that you could use to teach the strategy. Figure 4.1 outlines why you might choose a specific teaching method.

Teaching Method	Why You Might Choose to Use It
Class Conversations and Conferences  	Class conversations are opportunities for the teacher (or even children) to share an issue they've been noticing and ask for feedback and ideas for how to address it. Similarly, a conference is an opportunity for a teacher and student(s) to talk through an issue or idea in a smaller setting. Class conversations or small group/individual conferences are helpful teaching methods when you want to co-construct strategies together with students. These often feel more like an inquiry approach than an explicit lesson.
Explicit Instruction with Steps or Strategies 	Explicit instruction is when the teacher teaches students the steps or strategies for a skill they've observed the students would benefit from. Explicit instruction is helpful when there are specific steps or strategies you want the kids to learn. While the strategies are designed by the teacher, there is still choice and agency for the kids in which ones they choose and how they embody them. Teachers might use invitational language like "You might try..." and "One way you can..." to convey students' agency in these lessons.

Figure 4.1 *Teaching methods and rationale.*

You might teach the entirety of a strategy in one day (Figure 4.2), or choose to divide it into smaller chunks to provide more time for students to practice individual parts (Figure 4.3).

Monday	Tuesday	Wednesday	Thursday	Friday
Teach Strategy Lesson 6.4: Ways to Share				

Figure 4.2 *A sample schedule for teaching a strategy in one day.*

Monday	Tuesday	Wednesday	Thursday	Friday
Teach **take turns** part of Lesson 6.4: Ways to Share strategy	Teach **use a timer** part of Lesson 6.4: Ways to Share strategy	Teach **make it fair** part of Lesson 6.4: Ways to Share strategy	Teach **ask to use it next** part of Lesson 6.4: Ways to Share strategy	Teach **make a sign-up list** part of Lesson 6.4: Ways to Share strategy

Figure 4.3 *A sample schedule for teaching a strategy throughout a week.*

ONE WAY WE MIGHT PRACTICE IT TOGETHER

If we want kids to become independent in using strategies, then we need to provide them ample, supportive practice to do just that. The *One Way We Might Practice It Together* section of each lesson provides an example practice method (Figure 4.4) and teacher language you might choose to use with your kids. This practice might occur right after you introduce and teach the strategy, or might occur at a later time depending on your schedule. If you notice the students aren't quite taking on a skill yet, incorporate more practice!

Practice Method	Why You Might Choose to Use It
Role Play and Scenarios 	In Role Play children practice different situations by acting them out. Similarly, with Scenarios, the teacher reads a scenario card to students and they discuss possible ways to respond or solve a problem. Role Play and Scenarios are helpful methods to make strategy learning more realistic. They're especially useful methods to use if not notice kids can articulate what strategies they *could* choose, but you aren't seeing them apply them to their own life.
Social Stories 	Social stories are short texts you can create yourself that provide a comfortable, predictable story that can be read over and over. Social stories are a helpful method when you want to support kids in understanding a narrative progression of using a strategy from start to finish.
Interactive Read-Alouds 	In an interactive read-aloud, the teacher chooses a book to read the class, intentionally choosing stopping points along the way for discussion. Interactive read-alouds are a helpful method for kids to try out or learn about a strategy in a safe way (talking about the characters instead of yourself can sometimes feel safer).

Figure 4.4 *Practice methods and rationale.*

ONE WAY WE MIGHT SUPPORT TRANSFER

In an effort to further release the responsibility of utilizing the strategy to students, we want to provide some supportive feedback. The *One Way We Might Support Transfer* section of each lesson shares one way you might try that out (Figure 4.5).

Method for Supporting Transfer	Why You Might Choose to Use It
Pre-Conference 	Pre-conferences are when the teacher and children talk through an upcoming situation and think of productive responses before experiencing it. Pre-conferences are helpful for visualizing an upcoming situation and anticipating what strategies will be useful.
Coaching 	Coaching is helpful to use when you think a kid might need extra support with transfer. You stay close by and coach them through choosing and utilizing a strategy.
Timeouts 	Timeouts refer to in-the-moment pauses (not the punitive-type timeouts) similar to what happens during a sports game, where teachers can stop and bring attention to a moment that might benefit from collaborative problem solving. Timeouts are helpful to use when you notice kids aren't using a strategy and you want to bring the moment to their attention and collaboratively pick and use a strategy together.
Reflections 	Reflections are helpful to use after a moment in which a child tried (or did not try) a strategy. You might use a Reflection to celebrate the use of a strategy or maybe a strategy wasn't used and you want to talk through a do-over.

Figure 4.5 *Transfer methods and rationale.*

Figure 4.6 *Mari coaches students on deciding how they'll share the Legos using a visual chart with strategies.*

REWIND/FAST-FORWARD

Have you ever taught a lesson and felt like it just missed the mark? I remember teaching a talk lesson to kids about revoicing and sharing someone else's idea. It was a mess. As I looked at the group, I realized we desperately needed to learn the skill of genuine listening before we could get to revoicing and building onto each other's ideas. We were missing a foundational piece and needed to rewind or back down the staircase a few steps (Figure 3.7). The *Rewind* section of each lesson does just that. It provides a few ideas of strategies kids might benefit from *before* the current lesson. Note that the *Rewind* skills are not necessarily prerequisites to the skill in the current lesson, but rather ideas that you might try if you notice students not taking on the skills in the chosen lesson.

The *Fast-Forward* section of each lesson goes in the other direction. You might notice that kids have control of a current strategy *and* would benefit from more development of that overarching skill. This section provides some examples of strategies that might be helpful next steps.

Embedded within the *Rewind* and *Fast-Forward* section are what I call "complementary" lessons. Sometimes when you are teaching a skill to the class or group of students, you realize that there is another skill, perhaps from a different perspective, that needs to be taught. For example, if one student is having really big expressions of emotions and is learning how to safely regulate them, you might teach the class how to respond in a supportive way when others are having big emotions. This not only provides helpful social-emotional learning for everyone, it also creates an empowering community where kids have the agency to support and respond to each other (instead of you, as the teacher, having to manage everything). This book is all about living in community with one another, which means we're not just focusing on the student having a hard time but rather the community as a whole. Figure 4.7 illustrates what lessons you might decide to pair together.

Strategy Lesson	Complementary Strategy Lesson
Ways to work through a big feeling	Ways to help someone else who is having a big feeling
Ways to disagree in a helpful way	Ways to disengage when someone is trying to argue with you
Ways to work through making a mistake	What you can do when you see someone make a mistake

Figure 4.7 *How to pair strategy lessons with complementary strategy lessons.*

VISUALS/ANCHOR CHARTS

Anchor charts provide a concrete way for kids to visualize strategies. They also serve as an artifact of learning. Each lesson in this book has an accompanying chart with ideas for how you might teach the strategies. You know your kids best, so revise and innovate as you see fit. Before teaching a lesson, think about what kind of chart you'll use. Do you want to co-create the chart with the students? If so, you might map out the layout on a post-it first and then create it with the kids. On the other hand, if you're planning to introduce the strategies all at the same time, you'll want to have the chart pre-made before teaching. If you're introducing parts gradually you might choose to utilize big sticky notes or use paper to cover up not-yet-taught parts.

Figure 4.8 *If you want to create a chart alongside children, creating a sticky note ahead of time with your plan (top left) is helpful. Alternatively, you can create sticky notes to add one at a time during the lesson (top right) or create the chart in the moment with students (bottom).*

Keeping our goal in mind—kids eventually utilizing these strategies independently—we want to make charts as user-friendly as possible. Including elements like drawings, photographs, minimal text, and kid language can all help make charts more accessible (Figure 4.9). Taking a picture of the chart and then printing mini copies for kids (Figure 4.10) to keep at their tables can help empower and remind kids to use them. Modeling how to use and interact with the charts is essential. Having the charts nearby during anticipated tricky moments can be especially helpful. The more tangible and visible we can make the strategies, the better!

Figure 4.9 *Two charts with photographs of students.*

Figure 4.10 *A smaller version of a chart to support a student during writing.*

ANNOTATED LESSON

This section orients us, as teachers, to what this strategy lesson is about and why it is important to teach. This section explains the reason behind the lesson and helps you decide if it might be a good fit.

This section provides kid-friendly language for what we're learning in this lesson and why.

There are many different teaching methods you could choose to teach each lesson. This section provides one way, with some sample language, that you might approach it.

110 Lessons in Community

Lesson 5.6 WAYS TO WAIT

In the words of Mo Willems, *Waiting is Not Easy.* Whether it's waiting for a turn in a game, a teacher's help, or in a long line at lunch, waiting can be hard. Oftentimes kids can get dysregulated while waiting and "get in trouble" for behaviors that emerge when we're feeling antsy or bored. We can support kids by helping them notice when they're feeling antsy while waiting and teaching them skills they can use to help them work through the discomfort of waiting.

What Are We Teaching and Why?

Today we're going to learn some strategies that we can use when we are feeling stuck waiting. Sometimes we're in a mood where we don't mind slowing down and waiting, while other times it can feel really hard to wait. These strategies can help us handle the big feels that can come with waiting.

One Way We Might Teach It...

Explicit Teaching with Steps or Strategies

1. *The other day I was walking up to the checkout line at the grocery store and the line was SO long. It wrapped all the way down the aisle. It reminded me of when we get to lunch and the grade before us got there a little late and the line is wrapped around the door. We turn the corner and feel that "ugh" feeling knowing we're going to have to be standing and waiting our turn for a while.*

2. *There are many times in our lives when we will need to wait. Today we're going to learn some strategies for different things we can do when we're waiting.* [Show or make a chart in front of class.]
   - Take a deep breath
   - Play a game (I Spy, Categories)
   - Do something else (read a book while you wait)
   - Talk with someone

Lesson 5.6 *Ways to Wait* 111

3. *When I think about waiting in that long line at the grocery, I realized I could have done something else to help distract me so I wasn't feeling so bored. Next time I think I'm going to keep my book in my bag and read a little while I'm waiting. Think about a time in your day when you have to wait. What's a strategy you might use?*

One Way We Might Practice It Together...

Social Story

One way you might increase the practice and support is to focus on a specific part of waiting that is hard for student(s) and write a book about that. A sample story for a group that is having a hard time waiting their turn in a game might sound like:

Sometimes waiting my turn feels hard.

When I get frustrated or bored waiting, I can pick a strategy.

I can take a breath and use a fidget while I wait.

Soon it will be my turn and I'll be ready to play!

This section provides an example method you might choose to use with your kids to give them time to practice the strategies.

One Way We Might Support Transfer...

Pre-Conference

Think about times throughout the day you anticipate students might need to wait. We want to help students have strategies ready before they start to get dysregulated waiting. Maybe it's picture day and you anticipate students waiting in a long line. It might sound something like: *Today is picture day. There are usually a lot of people waiting to get their picture taken and we might have to wait in line for a few minutes. Let's look at our strategies chart. What strategy might you use? What materials or tools might we need to bring to help us be prepared?*

If we want kids to (eventually) become independent with the strategy, we'll want to provide supportive feedback along the way. This section shares one way you might try that out at points throughout your day.

REWIND

What to do when you realize teaching another skill first makes sense.

- How to Notice When You're Feeling Bored/Antsy
- Ways to Take Turns

FAST FORWARD

What to do when you want to add in more layers.

- Planning Ahead for a Long Wait

This section provides possible strategy lessons that might be helpful before this lesson (rewind) or lessons that could come next (fast forward).

HOW MIGHT YOU USE THE STRATEGY LESSONS?

The strategies in this book can be used to support individual students, small groups of students, or whole classes. You can utilize the same teaching and practice methods regardless of the group size. Knowing each classroom schedule and structure is unique, the lessons are written with all components in one place so that you, as the teacher, can decide how you want to pace the lesson. While the lessons can be taught in their entirety in one day, in my experience, bite-size pieces of teaching across multiple days has a longer-lasting impact. Figures 4.11 and 4.12 illustrate possible ways you might teach the lessons throughout a week.

Time of Day	Monday	Tuesday	Wednesday	Thursday	Friday
SEL/Play	Teach strategy lesson	Practice strategy (role play)	Practice strategy (role play)		
Literacy				Practice strategy (interactive read-aloud)	
Throughout the Day	Supporting transfer				

Figure 4.11 *A sample schedule (with a designated time for social-emotional learning).*

	Monday	Tuesday	Wednesday	Thursday	Friday
Morning Meeting	Teach one part of the lesson strategy	Teach another part of the lesson strategy	Teach one part of the lesson strategy	Teach one part of the lesson strategy	
Literacy					Practice strategy (interactive read-aloud)
Throughout the day	Supporting transfer				

Figure 4.12 *A sample schedule (without designated social-emotional learning block).*

A note about practice. While role play and scenarios, social stories, and interactive read-alouds provide specifically designed opportunities for students to practice strategies without the "in the moment" pressures, they are not the only times kids will have to practice. If you don't have designated time to practice, think about how you might intentionally embed opportunities throughout the day. Kids who are learning how to work together can practice this skill while playing a math game. Kids learning to work through making mistakes can practice during writing time. Kids learning ways to include others can practice this during a morning meeting activity. You can intentionally create opportunities for kids to choose their own partnerships for a project when they're learning about including others. The more we think about social-emotional learning and academic learning as connected curriculums the more of an impact we can have.

Figure 4.13 *Two kids put what they've learned about working together into practice as they play a math game.*

LET'S DIVE IN

So, let's give it a go! You can read through Chapters 5–8 in order, or you can flip to Appendix B to think about where you might want to begin in learning about and selecting lessons for your class.

Chapter 5

Regulation—"I Didn't Mean To!"

It was a cloudy September morning and our clean-up song had just started to play. Matthew was deep in thought building his Lego boat. The timer on the song was ticking down and the kids knew that cleaning up and getting to the carpet by the end of the song was a shared responsibility. Majda walked over and reminded Matthew it was time to clean up. She offered her help and started to pick up some of the Lego pieces around him. Matthew instantly became agitated. "Stop touching those! I'm using them." Majda tried to reason with him as another kid came over and started to help gather stray pieces. Matthew's body was growing increasingly tense, and as he tried to add another piece to the top of his creation it crumbled apart.

Matthew started to kick and scream, throwing the remaining parts of the boat and any other nearby Lego pieces into the air. The other kids retreated, looking to me for guidance on what to do next. As they shuffled back over to the carpet, away from Matthew, he curled up into a ball, sobbing. The more I had gotten to know Matthew in the few short weeks since the school year had begun, the more I learned that his current way of handling big feelings was to release them in a physical way. When he was angry with someone, he would hit. If he was upset with how something he was creating was going, he'd throw it. Matthew was doing the best he could to manage the discomfort from his big feelings the only way he knew how.

I had heard about Matthew long before he walked through the doors of our classroom. Matthew was coming from another school and there was ample data and opinions coming with him, despite him being only five years old. Matthew was described as having many "tantrums" and "defiant behaviors." By definition, "...tantrums are biological states of dysregulation, not willful acts of disobedience," and yet the way Matthew was described was as if he was choosing to "misbehave" (Kennedy 2022, 149). We have a choice in how we approach situations like this. We can choose to believe Matthew is purposefully giving us a hard time, or, we can choose to believe that Matthew is having a hard time.

WHAT IS REGULATION?

There are many different definitions of self-regulation. A more formal definition describes regulation as, "the act of managing cognition and emotion to enable goal-directed actions such as organizing behavior, controlling impulses, and solving problems constructively" (Murray et al. 2015, 5). In their book *Stop, Think, Act: Integrating Self-regulation in the Early Childhood Classroom,* McClelland and Tominey provide a helpful condensed definition, summarizing self-regulation as "the ability to stop, think and *then* act" (2015, 4).

When I first started learning about self-regulation, I thought this term was synonymous with being calm. Think about how we see the word self-regulation show up in schools. We send kids to "calming corners" or we tell them to "calm down" and yet, there are many different ways to get ourselves regulated in ways that meet our individual needs. Additionally, regulation looks different depending on what we're doing. Think about when kids are running in PE. A regulated student would be moving around, likely with high energy. When we think about what regulation looks like it's helpful to see it as monitoring and managing our energy to match the environment around us.

So what are the skills that encompass self-regulation? Similar to the variety in definitions, there's a range of skills and categories that self-regulation can be broken down into. The Office of Planning, Research, and Evaluation for Children and Families (OPRE) categorizes self-regulation skills into cognitive self-regulation, emotional self-regulation, and behavioral self-regulation (Murray et al. 2015, 6). All of these categories of self-regulation require executive functioning skills. Executive functioning includes three types of brain function: working memory, mental flexibility, and inhibitory control (Center on the Developing Child at Harvard University 2011). Many of these skills and components overlap and work together to help individuals effectively self-regulate. Figure 5.1 lists some of the skills required of self-regulation and examples of how they might show up in the classroom.

As classroom teachers, we know regulation matters. We see how students with self-regulation can maintain focus, build strong peer relationships, and navigate school with more ease. But the effects of self-regulation go beyond what we see and feel on the surface. Research shows that "children who struggle with self-regulation skills have difficulty building and maintaining positive relationships, paying attention, following directions and controlling unwanted impulses, all of which

Executive Functioning Construct	What It Might Look Like in the Classroom
Working Memory	• Remembering single and multi-step directions
Mental Flexibility	• Maintaining focus • Listening to and following directions
Self-Control	• Controlling impulses • Utilizing regulation strategies when upset • Delayed gratification • Turn taking

Figure 5.1 *Some ways executive functioning skills play out in the classroom (McClelland and Tominey 2015).*

impact learning" (McClelland and Tominey 2015, 1). If we want to help kids learn then we need to help them learn how to regulate.

It's important to understand that children are not born with self-regulation skills, but rather they are born with the ability to develop and grow these skills. And these skills develop across a lifetime. When I sit in bumper to bumper Northern Virginia traffic, late to a meeting after spilling my coffee on my shirt, I am humbly reminded of this. While we can all benefit from building our self-regulation skills, it's important to understand which populations are most vulnerable for self-regulation delays. Biology, skills, motivation, caregiver support, and environmental context can all impact and potentially delay a child's ability to develop these essential skills (Murray et al. 2015). Children exposed to toxic stress, trauma, and adverse environments can have delays with these skills that affect development (Center on the Developing Child at Harvard University 2011). Additionally, individuals with certain disabilities like ADHD and autism may require additional support to develop self-regulation skills (Center on the Developing Child at Harvard University 2011).

Figure 5.2 *Mari sits with a student as they utilize a tool and strategy to help themselves get regulated.*

REGULATING OURSELVES FIRST

As with most things, teaching and developing self-regulation skills in children starts with us. Research suggests that, "caregivers who have strong self-regulation abilities are more likely to demonstrate nurturing and responsive caregiving, interact more effectively with their children, and are more likely to promote these skills in young children" (McClelland and Tominey 2015, 21). Developing our own regulation skills helps us be able to not just model these skills, but puts us in a better state to teach and support children with these skills. Souers and Hall share the advice, "when in doubt, shut your mouth and take a breath," reminding us of the power that a restorative breath can have on our ability to regulate our bodies especially in the most challenging of situations (2016, 69). Kids are constantly looking to us for intel on how to react to situations and the more we can provide stable, regulated examples, the better.

Take a moment to reflect on which situations in the classroom during which you notice yourself having a harder time staying regulated. What might be triggering about those situations? What are some strategies and tools you might be able to use in those moments to help regulate yourself? For example, I find myself feeling overwhelmed when noise levels get high. I'm a big believer that classrooms should be filled with talk and productive noise *and* sometimes I just get way too overstimulated. In those moments, I've learned that a deep breath, some sips of water, and telling the kids I'm "off limits" for a few minutes helps immensely. These strategies not only help me feel better, but also model and normalize for the kids what it looks like to use strategies to help yourself.

Adults can help children by co-regulating. This often looks like maintaining a sense of calm, moving our bodies down to the child's level, softening our expressions and bodies, and overall creating a non-threatening, warm presence. Sometimes just sitting by a child in silence and modeling deep breathing can help children start to regulate themselves. It's helpful to remember that there's a transition from external to internal regulation as children develop. For example, a baby might signal discomfort by crying and the caregiver provides the regulation (external) by rocking the baby. As kids grow up, they can learn (with our teaching) how to self-soothe (internally regulate) themselves. This development might look different for each child, meaning that for some children we might need to do more modeling and scaffolding before they start taking on regulation skills independently.

ENSURING DEVELOPMENTALLY-APPROPRIATE EXPECTATIONS

In addition to paying close attention to our own regulation, it's also important that we consider the conditions and expectations we have for children. My nephew, who is two, bounces from activity to activity. He'll work on a puzzle for a few minutes, move on to read a book, then scoot over to play with some Magna-Tiles all within a few minutes. We embrace this because we know that developmentally, these short few minutes of focus are appropriate for a toddler. If I told him he needed to sit at the table and complete all the puzzles before moving on he would likely show signs of dysregulation as my expectations would not be developmentally appropriate. The same is true for our students. When we see students getting dysregulated we want to ask ourselves:

- Are my expectations developmentally appropriate?
- Am I providing proactive supports to help kids stay regulated?
- What self-regulation skills might this student need us to teach them?

INCORPORATING MOVEMENT AND EXECUTIVE FUNCTIONING GAMES INTO THE SCHOOL DAY

If you've ever witnessed (or given) a whole-group lesson that has dragged on for way too long, you've likely seen the effects it has on kids. The group gradually starts to wiggle, stretch out, start side conversations. Watch any assembly for kids that exceeds their attention spans and you'll see the pulsing of energy arise. The kids' bodies are telling us that they need to move! Building in movement breaks throughout the day is one way we can proactively support kids with regulation and increase their ability to learn.

Traditional school schedules are not necessarily designed with kids' movement needs in mind. We have to think creatively to provide more movement opportunities in and advocate for what kids need. One way we can reflect on the integration of movement in our school days is to look through our schedules with the following questions in mind:

- When are kids sitting for extended periods of time?
- When might we incorporate movement breaks to proactively support students' regulation?
- Is there sufficient time for unstructured outdoor recess play?
- What times of the day do we notice kids having a harder time regulating?

Figure 5.3 illustrates what reflecting on and revising a schedule to make it more developmentally appropriate could look like. When we think about incorporating movement into our school day it can look a variety of different ways. Movement could be an informal quick stretch and a few exercises or a more structured brain break (there are many different resources online to support this such as GoNoodle). Movement might also look like playing a game to build executive functioning skills. Games like Simon Says or Freeze Dance incorporate movement while also helping to strengthen kids' executive functioning skills.

movement/
unstructured time

Kindergarten Class Schedule

9:05-9:30	Arrival and Breakfast	← add in play as a soft start
9:30-9:45	Morning Meeting	← Movement break (game?)
9:45-10:35	Math	
10:35-10:50	Intervention & Enrichment	
10:50-11:20	Writing	← Movement break
11:20-11:30	Interactive Read Aloud	
11:30-12:30	Specials	
12:30-1:00	Lunch	
1:00-1:30	Play	
1:30-1:45	Phonics	← Movement break
1:45-2:45	Reading	
2:45-3:15	Recess	
3:15-3:25	Snack	
3:25-3:50	Science/Social Studies	← Movement break (game ?)
3:50-3:55	Closing Circle	
3:55-4:05	Pack up/Dismissal	

Figure 5.3 *A revised schedule to integrate more developmentally-appropriate movement breaks.*

SETTING UP REGULATION SPACES IN OUR CLASSROOMS

When children are dysregulated, the behaviors that can surface are ones that often result in punishment, especially if a child's response is to fight or flee. And yet, when we are dysregulated what we truly need is help getting ourselves regulated with someone with whom we feel safe. Unfortunately, in classrooms where there's often only one adult in the room, it can sometimes feel impossible to meet all of the kids' regulation needs on top of everything else. These situations can easily lead to asking kids to go take breaks or timeouts just to help ourselves stay afloat when there are multiple competing priorities. *And* if those spaces are used solely as a way to send kids away, they're not learning the regulation skills needed to break this repetitive cycle.

I didn't really understand this idea until I met my student, Jacob. Jacob was always in motion. Sitting on the carpet with the group was one of the hardest parts of his day. Like clockwork he would start touching others, rolling around the carpet, chewing his shoe laces, and doing anything he could to stay busy. These were likely all adaptations he had learned to help himself discharge this built-up energy. In the moment, I struggled to see his behavior from this perspective and often sent Jacob away to the break spot in an effort to contain his energy there and in hope of him "calming down" away from the rest of the group. I'd watch Jacob turn over the timer at the little cushion in the break space and proceed to wiggle and make noises there. He'd come back to the carpet and the cycle would repeat again. The break had no impact on helping him regulate. I realized there was a mismatch between what I thought was a supportive break area (cushion, fidgets, headphones) and what his regulation needs were (physical activity). Jacob didn't need to move somewhere else to sit still. He needed a safe space to release his energy so he could come back ready to learn.

My experience with Jacob led me to reconsider what a variety of supportive regulation spaces might look like in the classroom. We ended up creating a movement spot in the back corner of the room with optional exercise cards (Figure 5.4). We taught Jacob, and the rest of the children, that whenever they felt that big energy feeling in their bodies, they could head over to the movement spot and help themselves regulate. Jacob began to quickly utilize the movement space on his own. When he finished, he returned to the group, sometimes a little out of breath, and was much more able to attend and learn. We shifted our mindset from a more conventional approach of pushing Jacob out of the group, to leaning into his needs and empowering him (Figure 5.5).

Figure 5.4 *A student using a breathing ball tool to regulate (left) and a student utilizing the movement break spot (right).*

Conventional School Response	Reimagined School Response
This might look like an adult sending a child to timeout as a punishment or sending the child away from the group to take a break alone.	This might look like encouraging a child to notice when they're feeling dysregulated and helping them choose a supportive space and tool that meets their needs.

Figure 5.5 *An example of a conventional and reimagined school response to behaviors.*

UTILIZING VISUAL SUPPORTS

It's important to remember that regulation encompasses a lot more than just impulse control and teaching kids to self-soothe. Regulation also includes utilizing executive functioning skills for planning, setting goals, thinking flexibly, and much more. Providing visual schedules (like the one in Figure 5.6) can help students envision what their day is going to look like and decrease anxiety around the unexpected.

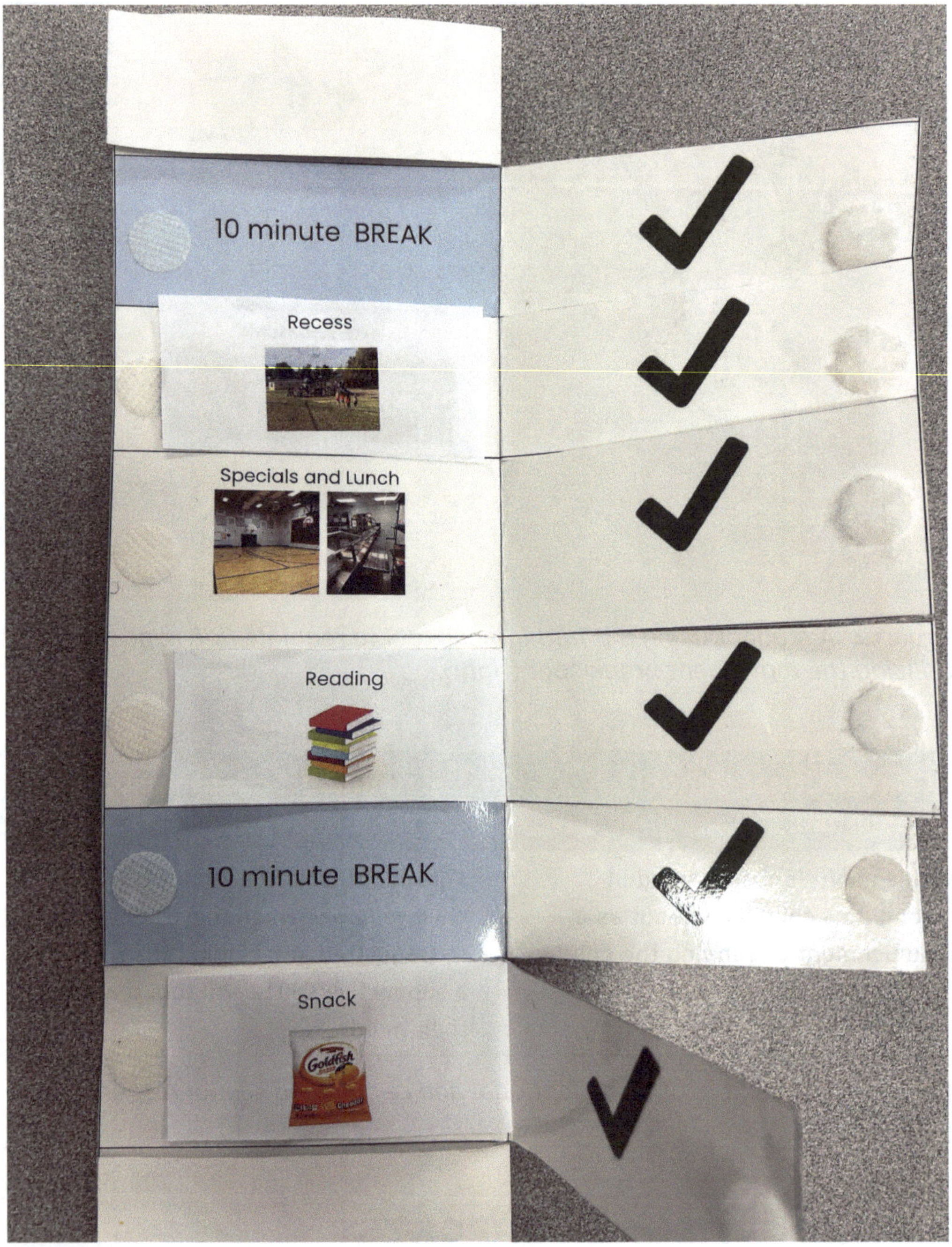

Figure 5.6 *An example of a visual schedule.*

When something does change in the schedule, like an assembly, you can update it on the visual schedule and talk to the child proactively about the change. This routine can help give kids a concrete resource to rely on when they're learning how to think flexibly.

For kids who are working on self-monitoring, planning, organizing, and decision making, simple visuals and checklists breaking down tasks can be incredibly helpful. Think about what the child might be having a hard time with and what success looks like for them with that goal. Then consider what scaffold or supports can be put in to help get them there. For example, a support for a child who frequently misplaces their glasses might be placing a simple visual placeholder on the table to remind the child to place their glasses there when they are not wearing them. A support could also look like a visual of tasks broken down into parts. For example, when I arrive I hang up my backpack, turn in my folder, unstack my chair, and then eat my breakfast. These visuals don't have to be elaborate, Pinterest-level works of art. I've scribbled many quick images on a post-it note that do the same job! Remember, our goal is to provide tangible support to help students as they work to strengthen their executive functioning skills. Over time we can coach children in making their own lists and visuals so that they can take that generative skill with them beyond our classroom walls.

It's important to remember that learning self-regulation and executive functioning skills is a normal and expected part of a child's development. While these skills may come quicker for some kids than others, all children (and adults, too, really) are in the process of learning these skills.

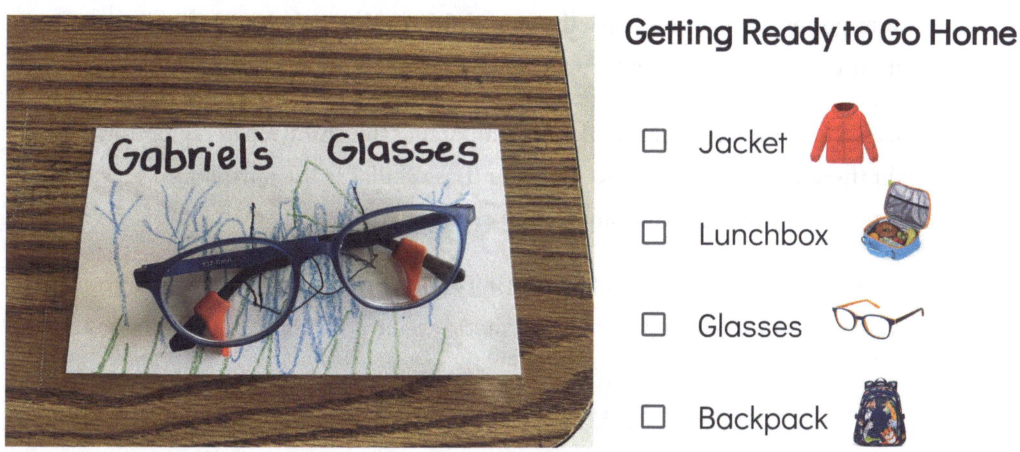

Figure 5.7 *Place holders, like this one on a table for Gabriel's glasses (left), and visual task lists (right) can be helpful supports for children as they develop regulation skills like organizing, planning, and decision making.*

A LESSON FOR OURSELVES

In the opening of *Troublemakers,* Carla Shalaby likens kids who appear to struggle in school to canaries in a coal mine, crying out to warn us of harmful conditions within our schools. She writes that, "our work as educators and as parents must become an effort to clean our air, instead of condemning young people, forcing them and actively training them to tolerate the poison" (2017, xxii). It is important to note that Shalaby's position is not anti-teacher or anti-school. She argues, rather, that teachers and schools are uniquely positioned to do the powerful work of disrupting the harmful systems they have inherited and creating spaces that instead support and nurture all children.

As educators, we want to widen our focus beyond just teaching social-emotional skills to the kids that are most obviously crying out. Our classrooms are ecosystems with many different interacting parts and it's crucial we examine all parts of the system. I often think about Shalaby's metaphor, asking myself, "How might the child's behavior be showing us, the adults, what needs to change in the classroom ecosystem?" How can we do the powerful work of 'cleaning our air'?"

In Chapters 5–8, before the lessons for children, I'll offer a repeated set of guiding questions. Reflecting on these questions on your own or with colleagues can help us consider the chapter's focus and what adjustments we might make to our classroom ecosystems beyond the strategy lessons.

- What parts of the physical environment might be impacting the child(ren)'s regulation? How might you rethink or adjust?
- How might other peers be impacting the child(ren)'s regulation? What learning might the community benefit from on regulation?
- What parts of the curriculum might be impacting the child(ren)'s regulation? Where might there be opportunities to integrate these skills? Is the curriculum accessible, engaging, and culturally relevant for the child(ren)?
- What is/are the child(ren)'s behavior(s) bringing up for you? How might your experiences be showing up in your interactions with the child(ren)?

GETTING STARTED WITH THE LESSONS

Now that we've thought about what regulation is and some ways we can support children in developing these skills in the classroom, let's jump into some lessons!

Read through the "If You Notice…" parts and you'll find some accompanying lessons and ideas in the "You Might Try…" section that might be a good fit. Lessons that are numbered are already created and available in their entirety in the chapter. Lessons without numbers are seed ideas for potential lessons that you might try creating in your own classroom.

If You Notice...	You Might Try...
Children seem unsure of how to work through their feelings or often get into a flight, fright, fawn, or freeze state. This can look like hitting, screaming, eloping, hiding, etc.	• Recognizing Emotions in Ourselves and Others (Lesson 5.1) • Noticing When You're Having a Big Feeling (Lesson 5.2) • Responding to Our Feelings by Choosing a Helpful Tool (Lesson 5.3) • Responding to Our Feelings by Choosing a Safe Space (Lesson 5.4)
Children get easily distracted. This can look like wandering around, talking to others, engaging when others are attempting to distract them, etc.	• Ways to Notice When You're Distracted • Helping Ourselves Stay Focused (Lesson 5.5)
Children seem unaware of their voice or body and how their actions might be affecting others.	• Understanding the Difference Between On-Accident and On-Purpose • Ways to be Mindful of Our Volume • Ways to be Mindful of Our Bodies • Ways to Tell Someone What You Need (i.e., space, quiet)
Children are having a hard time waiting (i.e., waiting for a teacher or peer's attention; waiting for their turn, etc.).	• Ways to Wait (Lesson 5.6) • Letting Someone Know You Need or Want Something
Children get disappointed when things don't go their way (i.e., losing a game, not getting to go first).	• Ways to Think Flexibly (Lesson 5.7) • Ways to Cope with Losing • Ways to Celebrate a Win

Lesson 5.1 RECOGNIZING EMOTIONS IN OURSELVES AND OTHERS

Our emotions often affect our ability to learn. Marc Brackett, director of the Yale Center for Emotional Intelligence in the Child Study Center, writes extensively about the importance of social-emotional learning in education. He writes, "the research is clear: emotions determine whether academic content will be processed deeply and remembered" (2019, 30). One of the first building blocks to building emotional intelligence with children is to help them recognize their emotions. Like most things, the first step is to notice!

What Are We Teaching and Why?

Today we're going to learn about emotions. Sometimes you'll hear people call these feelings, because they have to do with what we feel inside. Feelings are a way our body tells us information.

One Way We Might Teach It...

Class Conversation

1. *Have you heard the word emotions before? How about feelings? What do we think they mean?* Have students turn and talk and then share out to the class what they already know about emotions. Children will likely name some of the more common emotions (happy, sad, mad). Write these emotions on a chart as they introduce them. Encourage students to share about what that feeling feels and looks like to them. *Ooh yes, I've heard that emotion mad before! This is what my face usually looks like when I'm mad. Can you show me what your body does when you're feeling mad?*

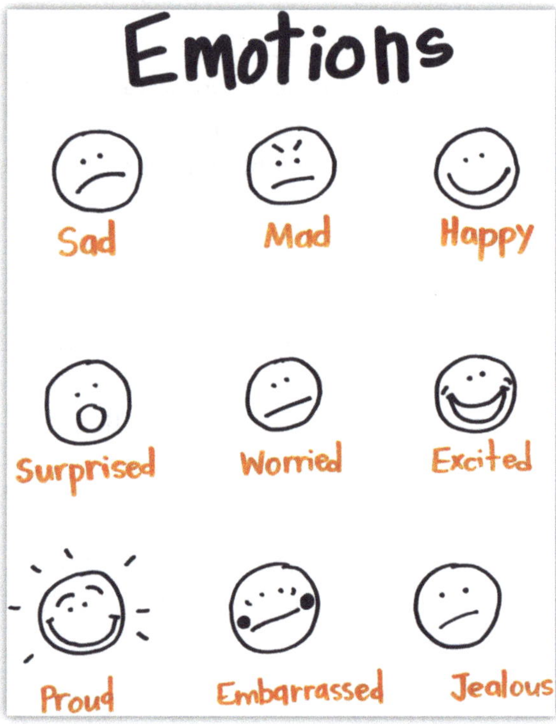

2. After the kids have shared emotions that they know, introduce other

emotions that the children might not have shared. *I'm going to teach you about an emotion that sometimes feels fun in my body and sometimes feels uncomfortable. It's called surprised. Surprised is when something unexpected occurs. I was surprised when my sister sent me flowers on my birthday! I was also surprised when a mouse ran out in my basement! Can you show me how you look when you're surprised?*

3. *There are a lot of different emotions! Throughout the day let's try and pay attention to what emotions we're feeling and see if we can figure out what emotions our friends might be feeling. We'll keep observing and learning about different ways emotions might look and feel.*

One Way We Might Practice It Together…

Interactive Read-Aloud

Today we're going to read a book called Little Faces Big Feelings *by Amy Morrison. This book is all about different emotions and what they might look like with our bodies.* Stop throughout the book and consider asking some of the following questions, having students turn and talk with a partner and then share out to the class:

- (Before reading the words) *Let's look at the pictures together. Look closely at these children's faces and bodies. What emotion do you think they might be feeling? What makes you think that?*
- *When was the last time you felt that emotion? What was happening in your body?*
- *Can you show us how your face and body look when you feel that emotion?*

One Way We Might Support Transfer…

Coaching

You're walking around during partner work time and see Jake rip a book from Archie's hands. You walk over and say, *Hmm, I'm noticing that Archie's face and body are showing he looks really sad after you took his book. His shoulders are down and he's frowning. Jake, that action really affected Archie. Let's brainstorm together what we might do next.*

Lesson 5.1 RECOGNIZING EMOTIONS IN OURSELVES AND OTHERS (*Cont.*)

REWIND

What to do when you realize teaching another skill first makes sense.

- Recognizing [a Specific Emotion] in Ourselves and Others

FAST FORWARD

What to do when you want to add in more layers.

- How to Express Our Emotions in Healthy Ways
- Responding to Our Feelings by Choosing a Safe Space (Lesson 5.4)
- Responding to Our Feelings by Choosing a Helpful Tool (Lesson 5.3)

Lesson 5.2 NOTICING WHEN YOU'RE HAVING A BIG FEELING

There are many different ways people respond to having big feelings. In some cases, this can look like a fight, flight, freeze, or fawn response. This might look like a kid fleeing from a classroom or physically hitting or throwing. In those moments, "...these behaviors show us that a child's body believes it is in danger and he is unable to regulate it in the moment, so he's reacting the way any of us would in a dangerous situation: fierce self-protection" (Kennedy 2022, 158). Kids are often protecting themselves the best way they know how. Where we come in is in teaching children more adaptive, healthy strategies for navigating those big, scary feelings.

What Are We Teaching and Why?

Today we're going to learn about how to notice when we're having a big feeling. We can pay close attention to what our body is feeling and doing to help us.

One Way We Might Teach It...

Class Conversation

1. *Have you ever had a really BIG feeling? I definitely have. One time I was building a shelf that had a million different pieces. I was almost at the end and as I was tightening the screw a huge piece of the shelf broke off. I was SO frustrated. My whole body got tense like this* (model tensing body) *and I screamed. At that moment my body was telling me that my frustration was building and I was having a BIG feeling.*

2. *Can you think of a time when you experienced a big feeling? Maybe you were feeling really angry or sad or worried. What was happening in your body? What did you do? Turn and talk with a partner.* As kids share out, record the different noticings on a chart. It can be helpful to remind kids that different people experience big feelings in different ways and even the same person might experience different feelings in different ways at different times. Here are some things kids might share:
   - Hitting or throwing
   - Yelling
   - Running away
   - Getting quiet

- Stomach hurting
- Heart beating fast

3. *Now that we have some ideas for what big feelings might feel like in ourselves, let's pay close attention throughout the next couple of days to our bodies and see if we can notice when we're having a big feeling or see another friend having a big feeling.*

One Way We Might Practice It Together...

Interactive Read-Aloud

Today we're going to read a book called The Boy with Big, Big Feelings *by Britney Winn Lee. In this story, a boy has big feelings and isn't sure if he should try and hide them until he meets a special person who changes his thinking.* Stop throughout the book and consider asking some of the following questions, having students turn and talk with a partner and then share out to the class:

- Before reading: *How does it feel when you have a big feeling? What about when you have a big feeling in front of other people?*
- During reading: *I notice he has big happy feelings too. Sometimes we just think about big feelings as ones that are uncomfortable. When was the last time you had a happy or excited big feeling?*
- After reading: *It seemed like during the book he felt like he was the only one having big feelings and wanted to hide them, but at the end his thinking about this changed. What do you think now about having big feelings? How would you want someone to respond if they see you having a big feeling?*

One Way We Might Support Transfer...

Coaching

You notice a student starting to show signs of having a big feeling. You might walk over and say, *I notice you're having a big feeling. I'm here to help.* If you've already taught some regulation strategies you could prompt for those. If you haven't taught them

Lesson 5.2 NOTICING WHEN YOU'RE HAVING A BIG FEELING (*Cont.*)

yet, you can lean heavily on co-regulating. Get down on their level. Soften your facial expressions and body. Remind the child that they're safe and you're here to help.

REWIND

What to do when you realize teaching another skill first makes sense.

- Recognizing Emotions in Ourselves and Others (Lesson 5.1)
- Identifying What Different Feelings Feel Like in Our Bodies

FAST FORWARD

What to do when you want to add in more layers.

- Responding to Our Feelings by Choosing a Safe Space (Lesson 5.4)
- Responding to Our Feelings by Choosing a Helpful Tool (Lesson 5.3)
- Ways to Help Someone Having a Big Feeling
- Ways to Ask for What You Need

Lesson 5.3 RESPONDING TO OUR FEELINGS BY CHOOSING A HELPFUL TOOL

All emotions are okay. Where the "not okay" part can come in is in the ways we sometimes express them. Kennedy writes about this saying, "after all, we can only learn to regulate feelings and urges that we allow ourselves to have; parents often have the goal of getting rid of the urge..., but humanizing the urge and then shifting where we allow a child to discharge it allows the child to gain regulation and, over time, make better decisions" (2022, 161). An empowering way to help children work through big emotions is to channel their urges and reactions into a safer release. So instead of kicking someone when you're mad (not okay), you might offer the replacement strategy of kicking or hitting a pillow in a safe space (okay). This honors the feeling and urges while also setting a clear boundary around safe responses.

What Are We Teaching and Why?

Today we're going to learn ways we can respond to our feelings by choosing a helpful tool. This is important because all emotions are okay, but not all responses are. For example, it's okay to feel mad. It's not okay to hit someone. Today we'll learn some safe ways to work through our emotions.

One Way We Might Teach It...

Explicit Instruction with Steps or Strategies

1. *Let's think about the emotion, mad. What are some things you feel like you want to do when you're mad?* Have kids turn and talk and then share out. Repeat with other emotions. *It's okay to have those feelings and even those urges to want to throw things or rip up your paper. And, we know that often doing those things isn't okay. So today I'm going to teach you some different strategies to use when you do have those big feelings and even those urges.*

2. When you're thinking about which strategies and tools you want to introduce, think about what you're noticing your kids gravitating toward. If you see children ripping something when they're frustrated, think about how you might integrate that into a strategy like ripping paper or using a mini paper shredder. If you notice students gravitate toward hiding under furniture when they're overwhelmed, think about creative ways you might support them in this like hiding under a blanket at the break spot. *When we're having big feelings, here are a few strategies we might*

try: [Show or make a chart in front of class.]

- *Moving our bodies (movement area, movement cards, walk)*
- *Curling up in a quiet space (headphones, blanket)*
- *Squeezing or ripping something*
- *Distractions that let us focus on something else (coloring, puzzle, etc.)*
- *Talking to someone*

3. Model how you might utilize one of the strategies. *It's time to pick partners and I really wanted to be with my best friend, but she picked someone else. It's been a hard day already and I am feeling really sad. Hmm, let me see what I need?* [Point to chart] *To move my body? No, that doesn't feel like the right fit. Curling up in a quiet space? Yes! I think I just need a few minutes to myself to reset. I'm going to walk over to the regulation spot and take a few minutes to work through this feeling.*
4. *Now we have some ideas for strategies and tools we can use when we're having a big feeling. Next time you're having a big feeling, think about what you need and try it out!*

One Way We Might Practice It Together...

Role Play/Scenarios

Let's try out some of our new strategies for responding to our emotions. Read some of the below scenarios (or even better if you create ones from your own class) and have students turn and talk then share out what strategy they might use to work through the emotion.

- You didn't get to see your friend today and you're really missing them
- A friend said that you can't play with them today

Lesson 5.3 RESPONDING TO OUR FEELINGS BY CHOOSING A HELPFUL TOOL (*Cont.*)

- You're trying to make a tower but it keeps falling over
- Soccer tryouts are this afternoon and you're feeling really nervous
- You lose the game you're playing during recess

One Way We Might Support Transfer...

Coaching

Keep your eyes peeled for big emotions today. Even better if you can get there before they reach a tipping point. Consider keeping a smaller version of the strategies chart with you today and when you notice a student's feelings starting to grow, prompt them to choose a strategy from the chart. It might sound like, *It looks like you're having a big feeling, did I get that right? What strategy do you want to choose to try?* If a child is already escalated, fewer words are often better. You might simply put the chart near them, reminding them of their tools in a nonconfrontational way and work on co-regulating.

REWIND

What to do when you realize teaching another skill first makes sense.

- Recognizing Emotions in Ourselves and Others (Lesson 5.1)
- Recognizing When a Feeling Is Becoming BIG
- Identifying What Different Feelings Feel Like in Our Bodies

FAST FORWARD

What to do when you want to add in more layers.

- Noticing When You're Ready to Come Back From a Break (This can be a great time to introduce timers!)
- Choosing Tools for Different Feelings

Lesson 5.4 RESPONDING TO OUR FEELINGS BY CHOOSING A SAFE SPACE

While it is our hope that all kids feel safe and comfortable in school, this is not always the case. It can feel really scary to feel dysregulated and navigate big feelings when you are feeling unsafe. For some kids, this can activate a flight response and can lead to kids eloping. While our hope is to eventually help kids feel safe enough in their bodies and classrooms that they feel comfortable staying and regulating there, sometimes we need to adapt to help them find other temporary spaces to regulate.

What Are We Teaching and Why?

Today we're going to think about some places where we feel safe. It's important to have places where we feel safe in mind, so that if we ever feel dysregulated and like we need to go to safe place, we can.

One Way We Might Teach It...

Class Conversation

1. *Have you ever felt dysregulated and had a really big feeling and it made you feel like you needed to run away somewhere? Sometimes when we're feeling overwhelmed it can be helpful to think of safe places where we can go. Sometimes those are in our classroom or homes, while other times they may be in a different place or with different people.*

2. *Let's brainstorm some places that feel safe and comforting to you.* Have the students turn and talk and then share out some places where they feel safe. If you're doing this lesson for an individual student, you'd write down the specific ones they choose for themselves. If it's a class lesson, you can highlight the differences in spaces

and bring awareness to how different people feel safe in different places and ways. Create a class chart with the ideas kids come up with. Here are some ideas that might come up:

- A break spot
- Outside walking or in the courtyard
- The counselors office
- Next to a friend

3. *Now we have some ideas for places we can go when we start having a big feeling. Sometimes we can go to these places right away like walking to a special spot in our classroom, while other places we might have to let our grown-up know what we need and wait a moment for them to help us get there safely.* If this is for a specific student who elopes, you might want to consider and communicate with the child the plan in place while they wait for support. This might look like them tapping and waiting by a stop sign at the door to let you know they need to leave. If waiting is hard, it might look like practicing using a tool (i.e., a fidget or something to help distract) while they wait for someone to come support them on a walk.

One Way We Might Practice It Together...

Interactive Read-Aloud

Today we're going to read a book called When Sophie Gets Angry - Really, Really Angry... *by Molly Bang. In this story, a little girl named Sophie has a really big feeling and when she has this big angry feeling, her body feels like it needs to RUN.* Stop throughout the book and consider asking some of the following questions, having students turn and talk with a partner and then share out to the class:

- Before reading: *In this story, Sophie gets really angry. What's something that makes you feel angry?*
- During reading: *When Sophie feels angry she kicks and screams. Look at the picture at how the illustrator is showing how she feels. What does it feel like in your body when you get angry?*
- After reading: *What are some things that helped Sophie work through her big angry feeling? One thing that helped Sophie was running to a safe space outside. I've had that feeling before and it can be dangerous to run off by yourself. What is a way Sophie could have gotten to her safe space in a safer way?*

Lesson 5.4 RESPONDING TO OUR FEELINGS BY CHOOSING A SAFE SPACE (Cont.)

One Way We Might Support Transfer...

Pre-conference

Pay close attention to the times when you notice a student struggling to utilize calming tools or strategies and instead resorting to behaviors like eloping. For example, if a student elopes every time it's time to go to specials, talk through how they'll advocate and get to a safe place. If the student is triggered whenever they're doing a hard academic task, talk through how they'll utilize a safe place. It might sound like *I've noticed when things feel too hard during math or you feel like you made a mistake, you run out in the hall and slam the door. Sometimes when we're having really big feelings like that we want to find a place to process them that feels safe. Let's think about if you were working through a math problem today and had that big "I need to run!" feeling—which of your choices would you choose? What would it look like to use that strategy?*

REWIND

What to do when you realize teaching another skill first makes sense.

- Noticing When You're Having a Big Feeling (Lesson 5.2)
- What Does Safe Feel Like?

FAST FORWARD

What to do when you want to add in more layers.

- Responding to Our Feelings by Choosing a Helpful Tool (Lesson 5.3)
- How to Return After a Safe Break

Lesson 5.5 HELPING OURSELVES STAY FOCUSED

Over the years I've heard many kids share their frustrations that "all they do is work" at school. I can empathize with them, especially as we move into the upper grades and the unstructured time available to children becomes less and less. It's important that we take this into consideration when building our schedules *and* there are inevitably going to be times when kids need to focus to help them learn and grow. Helping kids understand not just the benefits of focusing, but also the skills they can utilize to help them focus is critical. In this lesson we're moving beyond asking kids to "pay attention" and instead giving them tools *they* can use to monitor their own attention and utilize strategies to get back on track.

What Are We Teaching and Why?

Today we're going to learn some different ways we can help ourselves stay focused. This is important because focusing helps us learn and grow.

One Way We Might Teach It...

Explicit Instruction with Steps or Strategies

1. *Take a moment to think about a time when you've been trying to focus but were distracted. For example, the other day I was trying to read my book but my phone kept vibrating. Each time it did, I would stop reading and check it and get sucked into my phone and distracted from my reading. It was frustrating because I wanted to keep reading, but I was having a hard time saying no to the distraction of my phone!*

2. *When we're trying to focus on something, like I was with my book, it can be helpful to have some strategies*

ready to use when we notice a distraction creeping in! Here are some strategies we can try to help us stay focused: [Show or make a chart in front of class.]

- Find a good space
- Put distractions away
- Tell others what you need (*I'm trying to focus, can we talk about this at recess?*)
- Take little breaks

3. *I could have gotten a lot more reading done if I tried some of these strategies! Next time I think I'm going to try setting myself up for success by putting my phone in the other room and setting a timer for when I could take a break and go check my phone. What strategy do you think you might try today to help you focus?*

One Way We Might Practice It Together...

Role Play/Scenarios

Let's try thinking through some situations where we might need to really focus and think through what strategies we might try. Read some of the below scenarios (or even better if you create ones from your own class) and have students role play or turn and talk then share out what strategy they might use to work through the experience.

- You're getting ready for writing workshop and need to pick a place where you can focus
- Someone is sitting next to you on the carpet during the whole group lesson and they keep playing with your hair which is making it hard for you to listen
- It's independent reading time and your friend sits next to you and keeps trying to talk to you

One Way We Might Support Transfer...

Timeout

It's independent reading time and you notice kids are getting up and walking around. One student stops to talk to a friend on the way to the bathroom while another starts stacking their books to build a tower, gaining the attention of everyone around him. **You call a timeout!** *Timeout! Friends, I'm noticing some of us getting sucked into distractions and away from our books. Let's look back at our chart real quick* [Review

Lesson 5.5 HELPING OURSELVES STAY FOCUSED (*Cont.*)

strategies on chart]. *Everyone, pick one strategy they're going to have ready if a distraction comes your way.*

REWIND

What to do when you realize teaching another skill first makes sense.

- How to Notice When You're Distracted
- Identifying Times When It's Important to Focus

FAST FORWARD

What to do when you want to add in more layers.

- What to Do When Someone Is Distracting You

Lesson 5.6 WAYS TO WAIT

In the words of Mo Willems, *Waiting Is Not Easy.* Whether it's waiting for a turn in a game, a teacher's help, or in a long line at lunch, waiting can be hard. Oftentimes kids can get dysregulated while waiting and "get in trouble" for behaviors that emerge when we're feeling antsy or bored. We can support kids by helping them notice when they're feeling antsy while waiting and teaching them skills they can use to help them work through the discomfort of waiting.

What Are We Teaching and Why?

Today we're going to learn some strategies that we can use when we are feeling stuck waiting. Sometimes we're in a mood where we don't mind slowing down and waiting, while other times it can feel really hard to wait. These strategies can help us handle the big feels that can come with waiting.

One Way We Might Teach It...

Explicit Teaching with Steps or Strategies

1. *The other day I was walking up to the checkout line at the grocery store and the line was SO long. It wrapped all the way down the aisle. It reminded me of when we get to lunch and the grade before us got there a little late and the line is wrapped around the door. We turn the corner and feel that "ugh" feeling knowing we're going to have to be standing and waiting our turn for a while.*

2. *There are many times in our lives when we will need to wait. Today we're going to learn some strategies for different things we can do when we're waiting.* [Show or make a chart in front of class.]
   - Take a deep breath
   - Play a game (I Spy, Categories)
   - Do something else (read a book while you wait)
   - Talk with someone

3. *When I think about waiting in that long line at the grocery, I realized I could have done something else to help distract me so I wasn't feeling so bored. Next time I think I'm going to keep my book in my bag and read a little while I'm waiting. Think about a time in your day when you have to wait. What's a strategy you might use?*

One Way We Might Practice It Together…

Social Story

One way you might increase the practice and support is to focus on a specific part of waiting that is hard for student(s) and write a book about that. A sample story for a group that is having a hard time waiting their turn in a game might sound like:

Sometimes waiting my turn feels hard.

When I get frustrated or bored waiting, I can pick a strategy.

I can take a breath and use a fidget while I wait.

Soon it will be my turn and I'll be ready to play!

One Way We Might Support Transfer…

Pre-Conference

Think about times throughout the day you anticipate students might need to wait. We want to help students have strategies ready before they start to get dysregulated waiting. Maybe it's picture day and you anticipate students waiting in a long line. It might sound something like: *Today is picture day. There are usually a lot of people waiting to get their picture taken and we might have to wait in line for a few minutes. Let's look at our strategies chart. What strategy might you use? What materials or tools might we need to bring to help us be prepared?*

REWIND

What to do when you realize teaching another skill first makes sense.

- How to Notice When You're Feeling Bored/Antsy
- Ways to Take Turns

FAST FORWARD

What to do when you want to add in more layers.

- Planning Ahead for a Long Wait

Lesson 5.7 WAYS TO THINK FLEXIBLY

It's hard to not get what you want or for things not to go your way. Ask any kindergartener who's learning to navigate the tricky new world of having only one line leader and twenty plus candidates for the job. We want to recognize these sometimes uncomfortable feelings of disappointment and frustration and also help them build their flexibility and resiliency skills to work through them.

What Are We Teaching and Why?

Today we're going to learn some strategies we can use when we get stuck. This can happen when something isn't going the way we wanted or expected. Sometimes a little voice creeps in that says "things never go my way!" and that can feel really discouraging. These strategies can help us work through those feelings of disappointment and have a flexible mindset.

One Way We Might Teach It…

Explicit Instruction with Steps or Strategies-

1. *The other day I was painting with watercolors. I was trying to make my mom's favorite flowers on a card as a gift for her. It was going well until I put too much water on my brush and when it touched the paper it washed away one of the flowers, making it bleed into the others. It quickly became this big blob of purples and blacks in the middle of the page. I was devastated. This voice inside me started to say, "watercolors never work out for me!" Has something like that ever happened to you?*
2. *Sometimes in life, like when we're creating something or playing a game, things can go a different way than we expected and that can feel so*

frustrating. The first thing we can do is take a deep breath. This can help us reset and get our minds ready to choose a strategy to help ourselves. After we take a breath we can pick a strategy: [Show or make a chart in front of class.]

1. *Take a deep breath*
2. *Pick a strategy*
   - Self-talk *Maybe next time!*
   - Try it again
   - Try something different
   - Take a break

3. *When I was looking at the watercolors blurred altogether I had a choice. I could have ripped up the paper and thrown away the project. Instead, I chose to try it a different way. I got a smaller brush (to avoid any big water spills) and used a paper towel to dab it before I touched the paper. It worked! They weren't perfect, but I finished the project and was proud of myself for sticking with it. Which one of these strategies for being flexible might you try together when something doesn't go quite the way you expected?*

One Way We Might Practice It Together...

Social Story

You want to use language and visuals or photos that make sense for the student(s) you're working with (as in Figures 3.12 and 3.13). Here is one example of what the language could sound like in the story:

Sometimes things don't go the way we want them to.

Sometimes this makes us feel frustrated or sad.

We can take a deep breath.

Then we can pick a strategy to help us.

It can feel good to help ourselves work through a big feeling!

One Way We Might Support Transfer...

Pre-Coaching

Today is another rainy day, which means we're going to have indoor recess. During indoor recess a lot of you like to play games together. Sometimes when we play games things go the way we want; we win and that can feel good. Sometimes when we play

Lesson 5.7 WAYS TO THINK FLEXIBLY (*Cont.*)

games we don't win or we lose a turn and sometimes that can feel uncomfortable. Let's read through our strategies we can use before we go off and play. Think to yourself, what's a strategy you might try? What might you say to a friend who is having a hard time?

REWIND

What to do when you realize teaching another skill first makes sense.

- How to Pause and Take a Deep Breath When You're Having a Big Feeling

FAST FORWARD

What to do when you want to add in more layers.

- Ways We Can Help Others When Things Don't Go the Way They Expected

Chapter 6

Relationships—"You're Not My Friend Anymore"

Caitlin, Jasmine, and Reha were the best of friends and the worst of friends. Caitlin specifically appeared eager to stay at the top of their friendship group and could often be heard telling the others whether they did or did not have permission to play. Picking the class up from lunch was often filled with numerous kids fighting to recount their version of what was said, who hurt whose feelings, and which friendships had ended in the mere thirty minutes they'd been in the cafeteria. We often needed to have class meetings afterward where we talked about what it meant to be kind friends. The girls would scowl at each other from across the carpet. I'd insist they give (performative) apologies and we would move on.

A short while after lunch we would head out to recess. One day, only a few minutes after we'd arrived on the playground, Jasmine came running up to me saying that Caitlin said she couldn't play with her. Caitlin rushed over behind Jasmine explaining breathlessly that she and Reha were playing a game that could only have two players. Jasmine responded angrily and the two girls started to argue about what was said. "That's not true!" Jasmine yelled. "She's lying! She's just trying to get me in trouble" Caitlin hurled back. I took a deep breath and told both girls to take some space and play with other people at recess for that day. I knew it was a band-aid response, but I was exhausted from playing referee and needed time to regroup.

These kinds of friendship challenges are not uncommon in elementary school (and beyond!). While relationships come with great benefits, they can also come with disagreements and heartache. In extreme instances, lack of relationship skills can result in bullying and isolation. So often in schools we attempt to combat gaps in these social skills with initiatives that simply *tell* kids to be nice or kind and yet those reminders don't actually *teach* kids the skills they need to develop, navigate, and repair friendships. Caitlin, Jasmine, and Reha didn't need me to tell them to be nice, they needed me to teach them the skills to see others' perspectives, set boundaries, and feel safe and confident enough to repair when there had been a rupture in their friendship.

STUDYING FRIENDSHIP

Friendship is a concept that we could study for years. Our understanding of it grows and changes as we have different experiences and enter different stages of life. It

Element of Friendship	Primary Read-Alouds	Upper Read-Alouds
Friends trust each other	• *Elephant & Piggie* series by Mo Willems • *Help! A Story of Friendship* by Holly Keller • *Maddi's Fridge* by Lois Brandt	• *Cat Kid Comic Club* series by Dav Pilkey • *The Baby-Sitters Club* graphic novel series based on the novels by Ann M. Martin
Friends are empathetic	• *I Walk with Vanessa* by Kerascoët • *The Invisible Boy* by Trudy Ludwig • *Seeking Best Friend* by Alison Marcotte	• *The Hundred Dresses* by Eleanor Estes • *Wonder* by R.J. Palacio
Friends support and stand-up for each other	• *One* by Kathryn Otoshi • *Princess Truly: I Am a Good Friend* by Kelly Greenawalt	• *Before the Ever After* by Jacqueline Woodson • *Friendship War* by Andrew Clements
Friends give and take (reciprocity)	• *The Little Red Hen* • *Boy and Bot* by Ame Dyckman • *A Sick Day for Amos McGee* by Philip C. Stead	• *Pizza & Taco* series by Stephen Shaskan • *Beak & Ally: Unlikely Friends* by Norm Feu
Friends can agree and disagree (can be the same or different)	• *The Rabbit Listened* by Cori Doerrfeld • *How to Apologize* by David LaRochelle • *Can I Play Too?* By Samantha Cotterill • *I Can Say No* by Jenny Simmons	• *The Baby-Sitters Club: Claudia and the New Girl* by Ann M. Martin • *Freestyle* by Gale Galligan
Friendships can change	• *Friends Are Forever* by Diane Liu • *Evelyn Del Rey Is Moving Away* by Meg Medina	• *Hoops* by Matt Tavares • *Real Friends* by Shannon Hale • *Absolutely Nat* by Maria Scrivan

Figure 6.1 *Book list for various elements of friendship.*

can be helpful to spend time as a class thinking about and developing a common language of what friendship means to us. This study of friendship can provide a great base for teaching the lessons and strategies in this chapter. Whenever I want to spend some time digging into a social-emotional topic together I think about where we can integrate it into our existing curriculum. Studying a topic like friendship can often be worked into literacy. You can maintain many of the same objectives for comprehension, vocabulary, oral language, and many more while supplementing the texts in your curriculum with intentionally selected ones about friendship. The chart in Figure 6.1 provides some book suggestions for both primary and upper grades based on elements of friendship you might study and discuss. This is far from an exhaustive list and truly there could be entire professional books written on helping children navigate friendships at school. As this is just a snippet, consider what other elements of friendships you might add and what additional books you could include.

Figure 6.2 *A class-created list of what feels good in friendship (left) and a basket of friendship books added to the classroom library (right).*

HOW RELATIONSHIPS CREATE A SENSE OF BELONGING

As humans, we are social beings. It's in our nature to find safety and comfort through relationships with others. Souers and Hall write, "When we feel connected in a healthy way, we feel safe. When we feel safe, we can learn" (2018, 77). It's important to note that this doesn't mean schools have to be a utopia where everyone gets along, but rather that there should be value placed on fostering healthy connections in the classroom. As educators we must create safe places for children to learn about and grow in their relationships with others. And we must expect and lean into the difficult moments along the way as they tackle both the beauty and challenges of friendship.

Figure 6.3 *Two kids work together to build a tower out of Magna-Tiles.*

MODELING HEALTHY RELATIONSHIPS

As with most things, a strong model or example of what something looks like can serve as a helpful guide. Relationships are no different. Kids need (and deserve) to experience healthy relationships. This means that we must practice what we preach. If we want kids to listen to each other, we have the responsibility to model authentic listening with them. If we hope to teach students about how tone can impact communication, we want to be mindful of the tone we use with kids. I'll never forget my first year teaching, watching the kids "play school" during indoor recess and getting a front row seat to how they were interpreting my words and body language. While there were parts that made me cringe, this experience did help me reflect on my tone and body language.

Another essential (and vulnerable) part of modeling healthy relationships is modeling repair. All relationships inevitably come with their fair share of bumps in the road. As a teacher, it can feel incredibly vulnerable to apologize and repair with students. The (even subconscious) perspective that teachers are "all-knowing" can position teachers as infallible which can make repairing feel like a divergence from this identity. And yet, repairs are essential to building a strong connection. Kennedy writes, "I often think that healthy relationships are defined not by a lack of rupture but by how well we repair," solidifying the importance of teaching children how to engage in healthy repair work (2022, 137).

PERSPECTIVE TAKING

Perspective taking is an integral part of regulation and building connections with others. Ellen Galinski, author of *Mind in the Making,* describes perspective taking as

> the intellectual skill of discerning how someone else thinks and feels; it requires assembling our accumulated knowledge of that person, analyzing the situation at hand, remembering similar situations, recalling what others have told us about such situations, putting aside our own thoughts and feelings and trying to feel and think as another person must feel and think.
> (2010, 71)

A common cause of rupture in relationships is the lack of perspective taking and empathy for another's experiences. Teaching kids perspective-taking skills can help them build strong relationships with an empathetic lens. These skills help them far beyond the classroom walls.

So how do we teach perspective taking? Well, first, we need to prioritize it. Galinsky encourages us to, "view teaching children to be with others as equally important to teaching them independence" (2010, 88). Oftentimes relationship skills can be described as "soft skills," when in actuality they are essential for individuals to be able to collaborate and thrive. In an increasingly polarized world, it's critical that we work to learn to hear others' perspectives, experiences and opinions.

COMMUNICATING

Communication is a critical part of healthy relationships. As teachers, it can be tempting to try and resolve friendship issues for kids or have kids talk through us (I'm completely guilty of acting like a judge and asking both sides to present their cases to me). While sometimes these teacher-as-problem-solver strategies can feel enticing as quicker, less messy remedies, they don't allow kids to actually build their own communication muscles. So, what does it look like to help kids develop their communication skills? Ensuring kids have time to talk to each other. Directing them to their peers instead of us. Standing nearby, ready to coach or encourage, but reminding ourselves to stay on the sideline. This might require some rethinking of community norms such as what our expected volume level is in our classrooms. It also might require some flexibility in the times we "allow" kids to talk.

As a teacher, I am pretty tight about transitions. I usually play a song that gives kids a consistent timeframe to cleanup, and I have a clear expectation that they are ready at their next spot by the end of that song. One time during playtime cleanup two friends were arguing with each other. I was so focused on the cleanup expectation that I interrupted their efforts to talk through the issue that had erupted during cleanup. The kids followed my directions and left their conversation unresolved, joining the class at the carpet where they sat glaring at each other for the better part of the lesson. I truly doubt they got much out of the lesson, and, putting myself in their shoes, I doubt I would be able to focus on learning with an unresolved conflict with my friend weighing heavily on me. Later, when I reflected on this moment, I realized that I wanted to realign my practices with my values. Now this looks like providing kids who might need more time to talk through something with a quiet space in the room to talk, often with a chart nearby to remind them of ways we can repair with our friends.

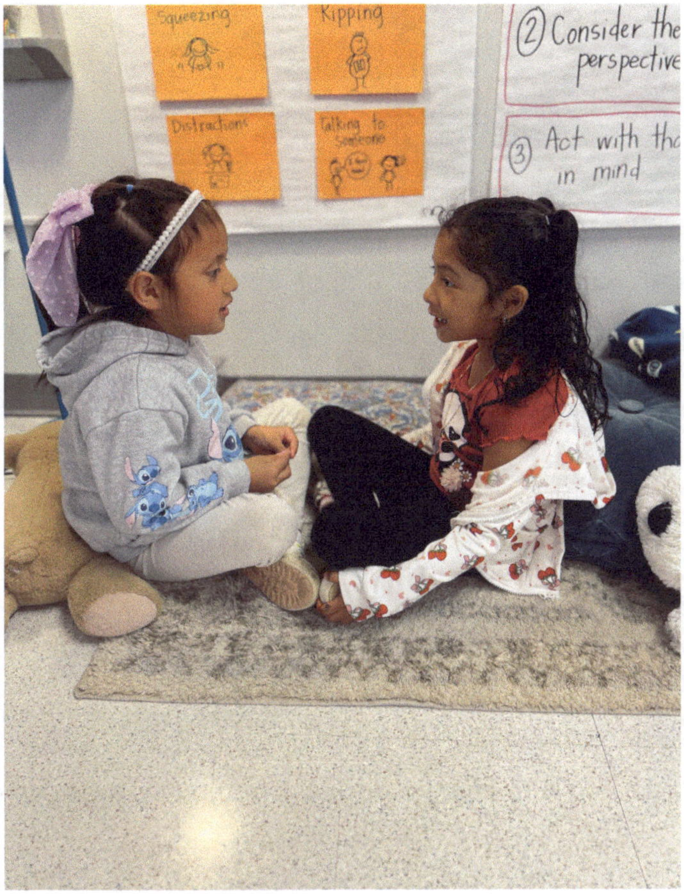

Figure 6.4 *Two kids sit together talking.*

SETTING UP A CLASSROOM FOR RELATIONSHIPS

The educational environment sets the tone for what happens in the classroom. We have the opportunity to create what Erica Buchanan-Rivera, in her book *Identity-Affirming Classrooms,* describes as "intentional spaces of belonging" in our rooms (2022, 103). When we design the physical space of the classroom, we want to think about creating opportunities for kids to talk to each other and develop relationships. Consider a room with desks in rows all facing the front. What message is that sending about how children are expected to interact with one another? Now consider a room with group tables and flexible seating. What message does this environment send about interacting with one another? Souers and Hall elaborate on this idea, writing that, "the way we set up a classroom, for example, can invite or discourage relationships" (2019, 78).

Figure 6.5 *A classroom with inviting flexible seating that kids can use fluidly throughout the day.*

In addition to creating an environment that invites interaction, we also want to be intentional about creating opportunities and structures where children can authentically engage with one another. Building in less structured time where kids can connect and talk, even for short spurts of time, can be helpful. For example, you might begin your day with a "soft start," inviting children to read, draw, chat, or play for the first few minutes of the day as students arrive and get ready for the day. We can also integrate talk and collaboration into academic parts of the day. For example, during the literacy block, you might have students read and talk about books with a partner. Buchanan-Rivera describes these critical spaces for listening and dialogue as, "catalysts for connectivity" (2022, 133). Not only are these talking and listening times helpful for kids to process information, but it gives them the opportunity to learn more about their peers and connect with each other. We can help students build connections and develop empathy as they listen to each other's stories and perspectives (Buchanan-Rivera 2022).

We can also get creative in how we support students in developing relationships. Buchanan-Rivera recommends kid-watching and observing the personalities and

Figure 6.6 *Two kids read and talk together about a book.*

interests of students (2022). Utilizing this information, we can form different partnerships and opportunities for students to connect around their passions and interests. Creating opportunities for kids to share about their families, experiences, and things they enjoy can help create natural connections. I remember when we were sharing All About Me bags in my kindergarten class and a girl pulled out a play caboodle of makeup. Everyone yelled, "Valery likes makeup too!" enthusiastically remembering that the day before a student had shared their love of makeup. The connections continued as kids bonded over their love of cars, books, games, and sports. Those conversations served as a catalyst for further conversations with each other throughout the day.

Kids also learn about differences through these activities. One time a student was sharing that they speak Arabic at home and another student asked what that meant. The student listened to the child's response, and then added on that they speak Spanish. Another student jumped into the conversation sharing that they wished they could speak another language. The discussion sparked curiosity and provided space to celebrate both similarities and differences in children's lived experiences.

Figure 6.7 *A child reads a class-created book all about what kids in the class like.*

A LESSON FOR OURSELVES

Before moving on to the lessons, take a moment, on your own or with colleagues, to consider the ways your classroom and school communities support students in building and nurturing relationships with one another.

- What parts of the physical environment might be impacting the child(ren)'s relationships? How might you rethink or adjust?
- How might other peers be impacting the child(ren)'s relationships? What learning might the community benefit from on relationships?
- What parts of the curriculum might be impacting the child(ren)'s relationships? Where might there be opportunities to integrate these skills? Is the curriculum accessible, engaging, and culturally relevant for the child(ren)?
- What is the child(ren)'s behavior bringing up for you? How might your experiences be showing up in your interactions with the child(ren)?

GETTING STARTED WITH THE LESSONS

Now that we've thought about some of the nuances of relationships and some ways we can support children in developing these skills in the classroom, let's jump into some lessons! Read through the "If You Notice…" parts and you'll find some accompanying lessons and ideas in the "You Might Try…" section that might be a good fit. Lessons that are numbered are already created and available in their entirety in the chapter. Lessons without numbers are seed ideas for potential lessons that you might try creating in your own classroom.

If You Notice...	You Might Try...
Children seem lonely, left-out or unsure of how to make friends	• Ways to Make Friends (Lesson 6.1) • Ways to Join in • Ways to Include Others (Lesson 6.2)
Children are having a hard time maintaining friendships or often seem in conflict with their peers	• What Makes a Good Friend • Seeing Another Person's Perspective (Lesson 6.3) • Helpful Ways to Get Your Message Across (Lesson 8.3) • Ways to Share (Lesson 6.4) • What You Can Do When Someone Doesn't Want to Play (Lesson 6.5)
Children have a hard time communicating clearly with their friends. It might sound like "you're not my friend anymore" or excluding others	• Ways to Talk to Friends • What to Do When You Feel Excluded • Ways to Repair (Lesson 6.6) • Ways to Share (Lesson 6.4) • Ways to Stand Up for Others When Something Doesn't Feel Right
Children are concerned about peer pressure and unsure about how to handle big problems	• What Problems Do I Need a Grown-Ups Help with • How to Cope with the Fear of Losing Friends • What to Do When Your Friends Want You to Pick Sides
Children get upset when their friend does something different than them. They're understanding of friendship is that friends need to like and do all the same things	• Ways to Disagree (Lesson 6.7) • What to Do When Someone Is Bossing You Around • Ways to Try Something New

Lesson 6.1 WAYS TO MAKE FRIENDS

For some, making friends seems to come effortlessly. My dad, for example, could walk out of the grocery store with weekend plans to meet up with the cashier he just met. Some kids can walk out onto the playground on the first day of school, meet someone new on the basketball court and declare them a new best friend by the end of recess. For others, this experience of making a new friend might look and feel different. For these more hesitant or slower-to-warm-up students, our well-meaning nudges to "go make friends" are often met with caution or resistance. These children have a lot to offer as friends, but may need more support in making those first connections.

What Are We Teaching and Why?

Today we're going to learn some ways to make friends. Sometimes friendships form without us really thinking about it and other times we might be interested in making new friends and want to learn some strategies for how we might do that.

One Way We Might Teach It...

Explicit Instruction with Steps or Strategies

1. *The really cool thing about friendship is that you get to decide who you want to be friends with and why. Some people choose to be friends with someone because they like the way they treat them. You might choose to be friends with someone because you both like the same things and enjoy talking or doing those things together. Today I'm going to teach you some different ways you can try to make a new friend.*
2. *When I was a kid I wanted to make friends and decided to try something new and join a basketball team. We practiced each week and I got to know the people on the team and ended up becoming good friends with a few of the girls! I'm glad I tried something new because I met some new friends I wouldn't have otherwise had the chance to meet. Trying something new is just one strategy you can use. Here are some other strategies you might try when you want to make friends:* [Show or make a chart in front of class.]
    - Ask to join something you enjoy (if you love playing soccer and see some kids playing, go up and ask to join)
    - Try something new (join a club, play with different friends, sit at a new table during lunch)

- Talk to the people around you (ask them questions, share about your life)
- Invite someone to join you (read a book together, trade Pokémon cards)

3. *Even though I was nervous to try something new, that helped me make new friends! Think about which strategy you might want to try and where you might want to give it a go.*

One Way We Might Practice It Together…

Interactive Read-Aloud

Today we're going to read a book called You Will Be My Friend *by Peter Brown.* This book is all about how tough it can feel sometimes when you're trying to make a new friend. Stop throughout the book and consider asking some of the following questions, having students turn and talk with a partner and then share out to the class:

- Before reading: *Let's look at the cover together before we start to read. What do you notice about the bear, Lucy's face? How do you think she's feeling about making friends? Now let's look at the other animals on the cover. How do you think they're feeling?*
- During reading: *How do you think Lucy is feeling now about making friends? What makes you think that? Have you ever felt like that?*
- After reading: *What could the other characters do to help include Lucy?*

One Way We Might Support Transfer…

Pre-Conference

Be mindful of less-structured times when kids might be trying to navigate looking for friends with whom to play. Consider saying, *Today when you go out to recess or to lunch, consider trying out one of our strategies. Maybe you'll ask to join the kids playing*

Lesson 6.1 WAYS TO MAKE FRIENDS (*Cont.*)

soccer because you like soccer. Or maybe you'll sit next to someone new at lunch and try to learn something from them. Remember that you get to decide who you want to be friends based on who you enjoy being with and who you feel safe with.

REWIND

What to do when you realize teaching another skill first makes sense.

- What Does It Mean to be a Friend?

FAST FORWARD

What to do when you want to add in more layers.

- Ways to Notice When a Friendship Isn't Feeling Good
- What You Can Do When Someone Doesn't Want to Play (Lesson 6.5)

Lesson 6.2 WAYS TO INCLUDE OTHERS

When we think about relationships and friendships, we often celebrate the boisterous, extroverted individuals and focus on getting the "shyer" kids to come out of their shells. And while there is great teaching that can occur around how to advocate, speak up, and ask to join, there are equally great opportunities to teach others to be mindful of quieter voices and take the time to value and include them.

What Are We Teaching and Why?

Today we're going to learn some ways we can include others. It can feel good to include others. We can also learn a lot from getting to know different people and their unique perspectives and experiences.

One Way We Might Teach It...

Class Conversation

1. *Have you ever seen someone sitting by themselves? Why might someone sit by themselves at lunch? Recess? Sometimes I like to sit by myself to enjoy a quiet moment after a busy day or I don't want to play with anyone because I'm too tired. Other times, I might be feeling shy and want to feel included but might feel nervous asking. In those moments, it can feel so good when someone invites me. Sometimes I take them up on the invitation and sometimes I say I want to stay alone, but it always makes me feel good when someone wants to include me.*

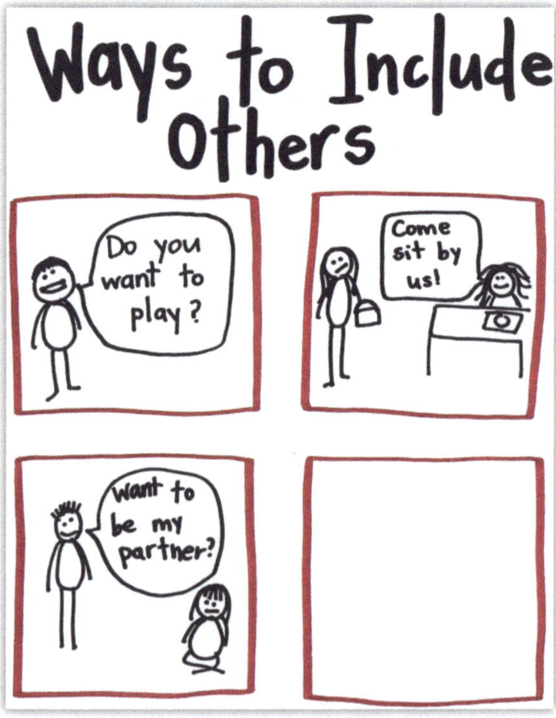

2. *Today we're going to talk about some ways you might try and include someone. If you were by yourself at lunch, what might you want someone to say to you? How about if you were at recess? What about when it's group*

time? Chart a variety of possible language kids suggest. Here are some examples of what they might say:

- Do you want to play?
- Do you want to come sit by us?
- Do you want to join us?

3. *These are great ideas for things we can say when we want to include someone and make them feel welcomed and a part of our community. Let's try this out today. When you see someone who is by themselves, try including them and seeing how it goes! Remember, if they say "no" it doesn't mean they're mean or that it didn't work. The goal is to make people feel included and offering does just that!*

One Way We Might Practice It Together...

Role Play and Scenarios

Let's try thinking through some of these situations together and how we might attempt to include others. Read some of the below scenarios (or even better if you create ones from your own class) and have students turn and talk then share out what strategy they might use to work through the experience.

- It's time to pick a group for science and you look around and see someone is left out.
- It's lunchtime and you see someone standing up looking for a group to sit with.
- At recess you see someone hanging out near the soccer field watching, but they haven't asked to play.
- You notice that someone's turn and talk partner is absent and they're not sure who to talk to.

One Way We Might Support Transfer...

Pre-conference

Think about some times throughout the day when you notice certain students are left out or there is more "cliqueiness." You might say, *We're about to make groups for this project. Think about what you'll say and do if you see someone who isn't in a group. How*

Lesson 6.2 WAYS TO INCLUDE OTHERS (*Cont.*)

might you invite them in? The more we can prime students with the language and tools right before these moments, the more likely they are to utilize them.

REWIND

What to do when you realize teaching another skill first makes sense.

- We Can Have Lots of Different Friends
- What Makes a Good Friend

FAST FORWARD

What to do when you want to add in more layers.

- Ways to Join in
- Ways to Stand Up for Others When Something Doesn't Feel Right
- Ways to Include Others Who Might Feel Hard to Work or Play with

Lesson 6.3 SEEING ANOTHER PERSON'S PERSPECTIVE

Perspective taking and empathy are skills that help us build and maintain strong relationships. Think about how you feel when someone shuts you down versus when they are curious about your perspective. The latter is much more validating and tends to build more trust and safety. Listening to others' perspectives and being open to changing our thinking and experimenting with new ideas and perspectives helps us in countless ways.

What Are We Teaching and Why?

Today we're going to learn about trying to see someone else's perspective. Everyone sees things differently based on their own experiences and feelings. We can try to put ourselves in someone else's shoes to see a different way.

One Way We Might Teach It...

Explicit Instruction with Steps or Strategies

1. *It can feel really hard to try and see someone else's perspective or point of view especially when we're feeling big feelings. And, part of being an empathetic, caring friend is to try and pause and widen our perspective. For example, I love the color purple and it feels important to me to have the purple marker, purple paper, all things purple! But, my sister also loves that color. Is it fair if I'm the one who always gets the purple thing? It makes me feel good, but then I start to feel sad looking at my sister. She's probably feeling really left out and disappointed. We can use the skill of seeing another person's perspective to help us develop empathy and be a good friend.*

2. *One way you can do this is by going through these steps. When you're talking to someone, especially when you or the other person are having a big feeling, try:*
    - Pause and ask yourself, *How might they feel?*
    - Consider their perspective
    - Respond/act with that in mind (*I understand you might feel...* or *How do you feel about the situation?)*

    It's important to note that sometimes we don't have the opportunity to talk to someone and hear about their experiences and feelings in the moment. In those instances, we can use the information we have to make a guess. However, when we do have the opportunity to hear directly from the person about their perspective it can be really helpful and lessen the risk of us misunderstanding.

3. *Remember that listening and understanding someone else's perspective does not mean we have to automatically do what they say or want. I can hear from a friend that they want me to sit by them during reading, understand why, and still know that it's a better decision for me to sit somewhere else. Hearing different peoples perspectives can help us see things in a different way and understand how others might feel. Let's try it out!*

One Way We Might Practice It Together...

Interactive Read-Aloud

Today we're going to read a book called They All Saw a Cat *by Brendan Wenzel. This book is all about how different animals see a cat.* Stop throughout the book and consider asking some of the following questions, having students turn and talk with a partner and then share out to the class:

- Before reading: Ask the students to describe how they see the cat on the front cover of the book. Consider asking them to share if they've seen a cat before and what their experiences have been. Highlight the difference in experiences, normalizing that each is okay.
- During reading: *What do you notice about how the [name one of the animals in the book] sees the cat? How might they feel? Why do you think they might see it that way?*
- After reading: *What did you notice about the different ways the animals saw the cat?*

Lesson 6.3 SEEING ANOTHER PERSON'S PERSPECTIVE (*Cont.*)

One Way We Might Support Transfer...

Timeout

You notice kids are arguing and talking over each other. The conversation doesn't seem to be heading in a helpful direction. Grab your chart and walk over and call a timeout. *Friends, one thing we've been working on is understanding other peoples' perspectives. Let's each go through our steps.* Encourage the kids one at a time to pause, listen to the others' perspective and consider or paraphrase what they heard. It's okay if the issue is not wrapped up in a nice bow at the end. Remember that the goal is not necessarily to come to agreement (although this is a great time to reference or teach a problem-solving skill), but rather to practice listening and thinking about another person's perspective.

REWIND

What to do when you realize teaching another skill first makes sense.

- Ways to Listen to Others
- Ways to Share Your Opinion

FAST FORWARD

What to do when you want to add in more layers.

- Ways to Ask Others What They Need
- Ways to Disagree (Lesson 6.7)
- Ways to Think Flexibly (Lesson 5.7)
- Ways to Share (Lesson 6.4)

Lesson 6.4 WAYS TO SHARE

Sharing is a hot topic in childhood. When I first started teaching and students would be arguing about a toy I'd often respond with something like "remember we need to share!" As the years went on, I thought more about the message that was being sent. Did I really want to convey that if someone asks for something you have that you have to give it to them? Or that when you want something from someone you should be able to demand it and are entitled to immediately getting it? The give and take related to sharing is an intricate balance and this lesson helps give some ideas for strategies kids can use to navigate these situations.

What Are We Teaching and Why?

Have you ever been playing with a toy and someone came over and asked you for it when you weren't quite ready to give it up? Or maybe someone was on the swing and you really wanted to have a turn? Sharing and taking turns can feel really hard sometimes. Today we're going to learn some strategies we can use to navigate those moments in a way that feels fair to everyone.

One Way We Might Teach It...

Explicit Instruction with Steps or Strategies

1. *When my sister and I were younger, we both liked to play the same computer game, but we only had one computer! We had to figure out ways to share that felt good to both of us. Can you think of a time when you had something someone else wanted or you wanted something from someone else?*
2. *When you are sharing with someone you want to make sure it feels good for everyone involved. For my sister and I, sometimes that meant we played the game together while other times, that didn't work for both of us so we*

decided to use a timer and alternate back and forth. It's helpful to have some different ideas for ways to share and figure out together what feels helpful for you. Here are some strategies you might try: [Show or make a chart in front of class.]

- Make it fair
- Play together
- Take turns
- Use a timer
- Rock, paper, scissors
- Make a list

3. *When we're sharing we can think about being flexible with the strategies we use. For example, it can be hard to make something fair when there's only one of an item. In those cases, we don't give up; we try another strategy! The important thing to remember is that we need to talk with the other person and agree on the strategy together.*

One Way We Might Practice It Together…

Role Play and Scenarios

Let's try thinking through some situations where sharing might come up and think through what strategies we might try. Read some of the below scenarios (or even better if you create ones from your own class) and have students role play or turn and talk then share out what strategy they might use to work through the experience.

- There's a new toy in the play center and you and your friend both grab it at the same time
- The class gets a new copy of a really good book and everyone wants to read it
- You really want to swing but all the swings are taken at the park
- It's time to turn and talk and you and your partner both want to go first

One Way We Might Support Transfer…

Timeout

Be on the lookout for situations where sharing comes up. Watch and see how students approach the situation. If they look stuck, consider calling a timeout. It might sound

Lesson 6.4 WAYS TO SHARE (*Cont.*)

like, *I notice both of you want to be goalie for soccer today. How might you use one of our strategies to figure this out?*

REWIND

What to do when you realize teaching another skill first makes sense.

- Noticing When You're Having a Big Feeling (Lesson 5.2)
- Ways to Be a Good Friend

FAST FORWARD

What to do when you want to add in more layers.

- Ways to Stand Up for Yourself and Others
- Ways to Speak Up When Something Doesn't Feel Right

Lesson 6.5 WHAT YOU CAN DO WHEN SOMEONE DOESN'T WANT TO PLAY

There's a delicate balance between encouraging kids to be inclusive and kind while also wanting them to stay true to themselves and make their own choices. Similar to how it can be hard for adults to watch a child react to another child saying they're not ready to share a toy, it can be tough to watch a kid bravely ask someone to play with them, only to be told "no." Instead of intervening and trying to sway the student to oblige their peer, we can teach children how to cope when someone says they don't want to play (or do something) with them.

What Are We Teaching and Why?

Have you ever asked someone to play with you and they said no? Maybe it was your mom and she said no she was busy or a friend at the playground didn't want to join your game of tag. When someone says they don't want to play sometimes we can feel sad or disappointed. Today I want to teach you some strategies you can use when that happens to help you work through it!

One Way We Might Teach It...

Explicit Instruction with Steps or Strategies

1. *One time I was at recess and I asked my friend Rachel to come play soccer with me and she said she didn't want to. I was so sad. I thought Rachel was my friend and when she said that, it didn't feel like she was being a good friend. But then I remembered that friends can like and do different things and still be best friends! Rachel doesn't really like soccer and when I asked her to play and she said no, she wasn't trying to be mean, she just didn't want to play. And that's okay. Can you think of a time when something like that has happened to you?*

2. *When someone turns down your offer to play together or do something with you, you still*

have choices! Here are some strategies you might try the next time someone says "no" to your offer: [Show or make a chart in front of class.]

- Ask someone else
- Ask them what they do want to play
- Try again later
- Play by yourself

3. *When we ask someone to play and they say "no," we can remember that there are other people we can ask and strategies to use! Instead of running to the teacher and saying "Isela is being mean!" when she says she doesn't want to play, we can pick a strategy to use and work through it. Let's give it a try this week!*

One Way We Might Practice It Together...

Role Play and Scenarios

Let's try thinking through some times when we might ask someone to do something and they might say no. Then let's think through what strategies we might try. Read some of the below scenarios (or even better if you create ones from your own class) and have students role play or turn and talk. Then share out what strategy students might use to work through the experience.

- It's recess time and you ask a friend if they want to come swing with you and they say no.
- You ask your friend if they want to come over to your house today after school and they say no.
- In art class there are different stations set up. You ask your best friend to come to the watercolor station and he says no.
- You're so excited to play in the kitchen today and you ask your friend to come play. They say no and go off to play with the blocks.

One Way We Might Support Transfer...

Coaching

Keep an eye out for situations where friends might be asking each other to join or do something. Hang especially close to children who have a hard time coping with the disappointment of hearing no. When the situation arises you might say, *Ugh, I know how hard it is when a friend says no. It can feel really disappointing. Remember how we've*

Lesson 6.5 WHAT YOU CAN DO WHEN SOMEONE DOESN'T WANT TO PLAY (*Cont.*)

been learning strategies we can use when that happens? What strategy might you pick? Consider having a version of the chart nearby for the child to reference.

REWIND

What to do when you realize teaching another skill first makes sense.

- What Makes a Good Friend
- Ways to Talk to Friends

FAST FORWARD

What to do when you want to add in more layers.

- Ways to Make Friends (Lesson 6.1)
- Ways to Join in

Lesson 6.6 WAYS TO REPAIR

Hurting someone, whether on accident or purpose, can bring up a range of feelings. When we experience uncomfortable feelings like shame, embarrassment, or regret after hurting someone, we often want those feelings to go away as soon as possible. Sometimes this can lead to brushing over harm or giving a quick "fake" (as my kindergarteners call it) apology to make the situation go away as soon as possible. But all of us who have experienced a glossing over or insincere apology know that doesn't help mend a relationship. We want to teach children not just how to work through emotions that come up when we've caused harm, but also the actions we can take to help mend and repair those relationships.

What Are We Teaching and Why?

Have you ever had a friend do something to you that you didn't like and wish they said sorry or tried to fix it? Or maybe you've done something that hurt someone else and you wanted to make it right but weren't quite sure how? Today I want to teach you some ways to repair things with someone.

One Way We Might Teach It...

Explicit Instruction with Steps or Strategies

1. *Can you think about a time when someone hurt your feelings or did something to you that you didn't like? Maybe they said unkind words to you or messed up something you were working on. It usually doesn't feel good. One thing that can help us feel better and mend those relationships is for the person who did something to acknowledge the hurt that happened and try to repair it.*
2. *Most of us have been told that when we hurt someone else we should say sorry. And that is one strategy we can use! But there are many other strategies*

that we can use to try and repair any damage we've caused. Sometimes you might choose to use just one of the strategies, while other times you might use a couple of them at the same time. [Show or make a chart in front of class.]

- Say *Sorry for* ____ (words or note)
- Try to fix it
- Ask them *What do you need?*
- Change your behavior

3. *There are going to be times in our life when we cause hurt to someone else whether on purpose or by accident. In those moments it's important that we don't ignore that hurt, but rather work to communicate with the person and use strategies to repair. The next time you bump into someone's tower and see them upset or you don't include a friend and see their disappointment, check in with them and try out a way to repair.*

One Way We Might Practice It Together...

Interactive Read-Aloud

Today we're going to focus on the strategy of saying sorry. We're going to read a book called I'm Sorry You Got Mad *by Kyle Lukoff.* Stop throughout the book and consider asking some of the following questions, having students turn and talk with a partner and then share out to the class:

- Before reading: *Have you ever had someone apologize to you by saying sorry like this: SORRY!* (yell the word and roll your eyes as you say it). *How does that kind of apology make you feel? Today we're going to read a book where Jack is learning about how to make a real, helpful apology.*
- During reading: *How do you think Jack is feeling? How do you think Zoe is feeling? How would you feel if you were Zoe and got that apology from Jack?*
- After reading: *What did you notice about how Jack's apology changed? What might we want to remember about apologizing from this story?*

One Way We Might Support Transfer...

Timeout

Keep an eye out for opportunities where someone's feelings get hurt or something happens that would benefit from repair. Call a timeout and encourage the students

Lesson 6.6 WAYS TO REPAIR (*Cont.*)

to look at the chart and think through what strategy might be helpful in repairing the situation. It might sound like *I noticed that (student) is upset about the words you said to him. When we hurt someone, we can think about ways we can repair with them. What strategy might you want to try?*

REWIND

What to do when you realize teaching another skill first makes sense.

- Recognizing Emotions in Ourselves and Others (Lesson 5.1)
- Ways to Recognize and Ask If Someone Is Ready to Talk
- Ways to Know When You Feel Ready to Repair with Someone

FAST FORWARD

What to do when you want to add in more layers.

- Ways to Ask for What You Need
- Ways to Tell Someone They Hurt You

Lesson 6.7 WAYS TO DISAGREE

Learning to disagree in healthy ways not only helps teach kids how to have productive conversations, but also teaches them to speak up and share their thinking especially when it doesn't align with what others are saying. Some kids are confident in sharing their disagreement (cue the "No, it isn't!," "Yes, it is!," "No, it isn't!," "Yes, it is!" back and forth) yet might benefit from learning more productive ways to disagree. Others might be hesitant to speak up and might need help coming up with ideas or phrases to say when they don't want to just go along with something or are feeling peer pressure.

What Are We Teaching and Why?

Have you ever gotten into an argument with someone who had a different opinion than you? One time I saw two people talking about their favorite football teams. They were getting so mad that one person started to call the other person mean names and the other person even pushed the other guy! They were not listening to each other or trying to see the other person's perspective. It is completely okay to disagree with someone and we want to figure out some ways to disagree in a productive, helpful way. Today we're going to learn some different strategies we can use to do just that!

One Way We Might Teach It…

Class Conversation

1. *Imagine that you're talking to a friend about who the best soccer player is. You say it's Messi. And they immediately shout back: No way! You're wrong. They continue to say things that don't make you feel good. Is it okay that they don't agree with you on who's the best soccer player? Definitely. Lots of people have different opinions on this. Is it okay that they're saying mean things over and over? Nope. They need to use a strategy to share that they disagree with your IDEA not mean things about you as a person.*

2. *Sometimes it's helpful to first think about things that don't really feel helpful when you're disagreeing with someone.* Call on students to share ideas of what doesn't feel good. Add those to your class chart. *Now let's think of some things that might be helpful. How would you want someone to respond to you if they had a different idea?*

Not Helpful	Helpful
• Yelling "No!" repeatedly • Saying unkind things about the person • Laughing at the person	• Ask them about why they think that • Share your idea "I have a different idea" • Say something like "It's okay that we both have different opinions," or "we don't have to agree"

3. *Let's try out some of these strategies and continue to add to them. If you notice someone slipping into the less helpful responses, encourage the person to try out a helpful way to disagree.*

One Way We Might Practice It Together...

Role Play and Scenarios

There are a lot of instructional practices that can invite rich conversations where students will likely have disagreeing ideas and opinions. Consider having a conversation in a morning meeting around a fun, low-stakes question like *What is the coolest animal?* or *Would you rather be able to fly or be invisible?* or playing a math game like Which One Doesn't Belong? or Would you Rather...? Any of these activities can create a scenario where students will have a chance to try out disagreeing in a productive way.

One Way We Might Support Transfer...

Timeout

When you notice students arguing in a way that is not helpful, call a timeout. Bring them over to the chart (or have a mini version available) and talk through how we can share our disagreements or different opinions in a helpful way. It might sound like *I hear you both arguing and starting to say some things that aren't kind. I also notice you're yelling at each other and that usually doesn't feel good. Let's take a breath and*

Lesson 6.7 WAYS TO DISAGREE (*Cont.*)

look at the strategies we can use to share our opinions in a way we can both feel heard and respected.

REWIND

What to do when you realize teaching another skill first makes sense.

- Ways to Get Out of an Argument
- Noticing When You're Having a Big Feeling (Lesson 5.2)

FAST FORWARD

What to do when you want to add in more layers.

- Seeing Another Person's Perspective (Lesson 6.3)

Chapter 7

Problem Solving—"I Can't Do It"

Ethan was a kid who felt challenges deeply. He was quick to get teary when he couldn't find a pen or was struggling to put on his jacket. One day at recess Ethan was eagerly running over to the swings and tripped. He fell to the ground sobbing. After being consoled by friends he got up and continued walking over to the swings, which were now fully occupied. At this sight, he crumpled to the ground, yelling, "this always happens!" through sobs. Friends eagerly attended to him again and encouraged him to join a game of tag. Ethan eventually joined in and began to run around with his friends. As he ran, his shoe slipped off. I braced myself as I saw this unfold. His eyes filled with tears and he started to wail. "I hate this game!" Ethan screamed as he threw his shoe across the playground. As I walked over to him, I empathized with how he was feeling. Haven't we all had those moments when something isn't working as we'd hoped and we just want to throw it across the room or drop to the ground in defeat? I knew we needed to validate these struggles *and* find a way to help Ethan develop the skills to confidently work through these challenges.

Before jumping in to teaching Ethan skills, I started to observe what response he was currently receiving when he had these struggles. When his friends saw him upset, they often consoled him and attempted to help. When he couldn't find his pen, peers gave him one. When he cried that he wanted the *Fly Guy* book, the other students would simply give it to him. Often adults responded similarly. When his milk spilled at lunch, the grown-ups cleaned it up. When he got teary that drawing a dinosaur during writing was too hard, a teacher would draw it for him. Everyone's well-meaning attempts to "help" Ethan also unintentionally conveyed that we didn't actually believe he could do it on his own (or that we were too scared of his emotional response). It started to click that Ethan wasn't becoming a confident problem solver partially because we weren't giving him the opportunities and coaching to see himself as one. Ethan (just like many kids) needed ample opportunities, encouragement, and reminders of strategies to ultimately begin to feel capable and successful.

WHAT DO I MEAN BY PROBLEM SOLVING?

It's important to note that the word "problem" is subjective. A problem to one person could not be a problem to another. I use the term *problem* here because it feels concrete and relatable to kids. Problems, in this sense, are not issues the teacher finds problematic, but rather something the child views as hard or frustrating. These are kid-identified problems. With that in mind, we want to tread carefully with qualifying problems for kids. As adults, what we deem as problematic and what isn't can be very different from how a child experiences them. For example, to me someone sitting where I usually sit in a meeting is not a big deal, but to a six-year-old this can feel like a huge boundary violation. We want to be mindful of honoring what kids see as problems and be cautious when categorizing their problems for them. At the same time, we can support kids in seeing the impact of their actions on others in their community when they might feel like something is not a problem.

In this book, problem solving is broken down across chapters. Problems related to regulation, wait time, emotions are in Chapter 5: Regulation. Problems around issues of sharing, friendship, arguing, etc. are all in Chapter 6: Relationships. In this chapter, problem solving is primarily focused on gaining new skills to be independent with either something the child wants to do or something we as teachers want the child to do (hopefully both). Many of these problems are related to developing physical motor skills. This is especially present in early childhood. For young kids that might mean learning to put on their jackets or open things on their own. For older kids this might look like getting better at shooting hoops or creating sophisticated friendship bracelets. Another component of problem solving here is related to developing academic skills. For young kids this might look like persisting when learning to write their name or count items. For older kids this might be sticking with a challenging math concept or learning to organize a binder in a way that helps you find materials.

GIVING KIDS OPPORTUNITIES FOR HEALTHY STRUGGLE

As we dive into teaching kids about navigating struggles, it can be helpful to reflect on our own relationship with mistakes and challenges. How do you feel about challenges? Are they an opportunity for growth? Worth the struggle? Or something we want to get rid of and avoid? Maybe a little bit of both? To me, mistakes and challenges can still feel icky and stressful in the moment, but by sticking with them through the discomfort I've developed confidence and new skills. The more evidence I have (and look for) of growth through effort, the more willing I am to sit in the messy discomfort.

Unpacking how we feel about mistakes and challenges and unpacking how that might show up in our instructional decisions is important. Teachers who embrace challenges often integrate open-ended, critical thinking tasks and creative projects into their classrooms. They emphasize thinking and growth over a narrowly defined end goal. And they expect kids to struggle some, to not know the answer right away. In our hearts and minds, many of us agree with this approach. But it's often easier said than done. Open-ended tasks can feel daunting, even overwhelming at times. The fear of the unknown and our own discomfort with students' productive struggle can lead us to more one-right-answer types of activities in order to avoid these feelings.

Dr. Becky Kennedy writes about this idea, encouraging us to shift our priorities to resiliency over happiness (2022). Oftentimes when we prioritize happiness, we can panic when we see or feel discomfort (that can often arise with challenges) and want to swoop in to remove the challenge or prevent the challenge in the first place. And yet, there is such a thing as healthy stress and struggle. Megan Gunnar, child psychologist and expert on stress and coping in children, defines stress as, "when demands on your body or your expectations of those demands exceed your ability to handle them" (Galinsky 2010, 250). Knowing this, our focus must be on building up kids' skills to be able to manage themselves in those stressful moments, not simply remove the stress and challenge itself.

When I think about healthy stress I'm reminded of Matthew, a student you met in Chapter 4. Matthew had a really hard time coping with losing games. I noticed early on that many of his teachers walked on eggshells when he would play a game. Anytime he would come close to losing they would intervene to add in another turn or change the rules so that he wouldn't be out or lose. Similarly, the kids allowed him to dominate the games. He'd intentionally "roll" a certain number with the dice to ensure he got a winning number or even switch cards when he anticipated he was about to lose. There was an unspoken understanding that we wouldn't rock the boat in an effort to avoid a big explosion of feelings. While I completely empathize with Matthew that sitting in the discomfort of losing can be incredibly hard, both as the individual and bystander, in never allowing him to have this experience we were robbing Matthew of the chance to learn to cope with the challenges. We were prioritizing happiness over resiliency.

Figure 7.1 *Two kids apply problem-solving skills while playing a game of Spot It! together.*

It's important to note that balance is key when considering healthy stress and challenges. Galinsky writes that when we think about stress we want to consider the nature of the stress, how long it lasts, relationships of trust with the child, and how caretakers are able to support the child through the stress (2010). We can support children in learning to manage stress in healthy ways, giving them some control over the strategies they choose in stressful moments and meeting each child where they are. In essence, we want the challenge to be within a child's zone of proximal development. This means that what might feel like healthy stress to one kid, could feel unsafe to another. Our level or support will vary depending on the child. For Matthew, learning to manage stress looked like teaching him strategies to cope with the uncomfortable feelings associated with losing and practicing playing a game in a smaller setting with safe adults first and then peers. Life is full of natural opportunities for us to practice skills and learn to cope with challenges. Additionally, we can support children with this learning by intentionally posing challenging tasks and games that provide opportunities for kids to engage in healthy struggle.

Figure 7.2 *A child uses scissors to work on a craft she is creating (left) while another child paints a self-portrait at the easel (right). Learning to take on new challenges and uncertainties is an important part of child development.*

THE NEED TO FEEL SEEN AND HEARD

Have you ever vented about a problem to someone and they say something along the lines of "Just keep trying!" or "Think positive!"? While phrases like these are often well-intentioned, they can feel invalidating and dismissive. Unsolicited suggestions and solutions can feel the same way. Often what many of us want and need first when sharing about a problem or experiencing an uncomfortable feeling is to be acknowledged and seen. There is great power and validation in pausing to acknowledge that sometimes things are hard and just feel crummy. When I spill my full, six-dollar chai latte as I walk into work I don't want to hear, "Next time maybe don't carry so many things at once," or "At least it wasn't a venti!" What I really want is for someone to look at me and say, "That really sucks."

Kids are often looking for this same validation. Ever watch a kid solve their problem and then come up to you to report the same (now resolved) problem to you? Sometimes these kids are labeled as "tattletales" or "being dramatic." Often what lies behind that behavior is the need to have their experience and feelings validated. Utilizing phrases like, "That must have been really hard," or "I understand why that would make you feel that way," first (or when they're retelling the story to us later) before jumping in to prompt for strategies or taking action can be incredibly helpful.

UNDERSTANDING THE POWER OF OUR MINDSET

One thing that can really impact our thinking and response to mistakes is our mindset. Carol Dweck, author of *Mindset: The New Psychology of Success* writes about two different kinds of mindsets: a growth mindset and a fixed mindset (2007). A growth mindset embodies the idea that your abilities can improve through effort. It's a malleable, fluid view on intelligence and ability. A fixed mindset on the other hand, has a much more limiting view, assuming that intelligence and ability are unchangeable. Think about a kid learning to tie their shoes. A student with a growth mindset might view it as a challenge that they haven't quite mastered *yet.* They keep practicing because they believe that the effort they put in can change the outcome. Now think of a student with a fixed mindset. They can't tie their shoes and believe "they'll never be able to do it" so there's no point in trying. It's important to note that mindset is also contextual. You can have a fixed mindset about one thing and a growth mindset about something else. It's not a permanent fixture of your personality.

It can be tricky to try and tackle working through making mistakes and problems when you have a fixed mindset about the task at hand. For some kids it can be hard to buy into trying problem-solving strategies if they believe they can't do something regardless of their effort. In these instances, it can be helpful to talk about the benefits of a growth mindset and really try to shift our focus to process over product. Shifting our language to "you kept trying and figured it out!" instead of "good job" underscores the importance of effort over fixed ability. Literature can be a great place to launch shared conversations about the idea that we can learn from mistakes and our brains can grow and change. Here are a few books that I especially love for this topic:

- *I'm the Best* by Lucy Cousins
- *The Girl Who Never Made Mistakes* by Mark Pete and Gary Rubenstein

- *Ish* by Peter Reynolds
- *Beautiful Oops* by Barney Saltzberg
- *Rosie Revere, Engineer* by Andrea Beaty
- *Salt in His Shoes* by Deloris Jordan
- *It's Okay to Make Mistakes* by Todd Parr
- *Abdul's Story* by Jamilah Thompkins-Bigelow

Another great resource for teachers to help their students build a deeper understanding of a growth mindset is Christine Hertz and Kristine Mraz's book *A Mindset for Learning: Teaching the Traits of Joyful, Independent Growth* (2015). This book introduces different mindsets and strategies for teaching them in the classroom. It's a great resource to lean on if you want to dig deeper into developing the skills of optimism, persistence, flexibility, resilience, and empathy with your kids.

SITTING ON YOUR HANDS—A GOOD FIRST STEP!

Sometimes just the anticipation of the struggle leads us to jump in before giving kids the chance to grapple with something and make an approximation. This can lead to us doing things for kids that they can learn and feel empowered to do on their own. It's also fair to acknowledge that jumping in is often ... easier. I remember encouraging a kid to open a packet of playing cards on their own at a math night at school and, as the child fumbled with the plastic, the parent looked at me and said, "I can't watch. You have way more patience than I do!" I knew exactly how the parent was feeling. It can feel so uncomfortable to witness the struggle! I literally had to sit on my hands to refrain from jumping in and helping. But here's the thing. As soon as the girl opened the package, she shrieked "I did it!" And then, as she smiled, she noticed another kid fumbling with the packaging and went over to help. For her, she just needed the time and patience to try out some different strategies and figure it out. Once she did that, she was off and running with the confidence to do it again.

Figure 7.3 *A student attempts to tie his shoe independently.*

As helpers at heart, sometimes the first step toward helping kids be independent problem solvers is teaching ourselves to step back. Teaching ourselves to take a beat before zipping a kid's jacket for them, telling them how to spell a word, or jumping in with an idea for how to build a stable tower that doesn't fall over. That doesn't mean we will never help a child again. Just that we pause and consider how we will help the child. And often, that means teaching them strategies that can help them both with the challenge in front of them and the many challenges to come.

Figure 7.4 *After a craft kept sliding apart, a child asked a peer to help her hold it together as the glue dries.*

EMPOWERING KIDS WITH TOOLS AND SCAFFOLDS

There's a fine line between not swooping in to save kids from challenges and leaving them hanging out to dry. So, what might it look like to support kids, without saving them? First, we want to think about how we are teaching our students to manage their stress and persist through challenges. Oftentimes our instincts might be to tell rather than teach. We might catch ourselves saying, "you can do this" or "keep trying." While words of encouragement are great, when we stop there we aren't actually equipping kids with strategies for *how* they can keep trying. This can lead to frustration when kids know that they need to keep trying and might even have the desire to, but don't yet have the problem-solving skills.

This can be especially tricky when a child wants to attempt something that might feel out of their reach or learn a new skill that might take them a while to develop. A sixth grader at my school, Kaitlyn, would often get up and walk out of the classroom when things felt too hard during math class. If the teacher could get to the door before Kailtin made her exit, they might be able to talk her into staying, but they also knew they needed to set up scaffolds for her in the meantime. Creating a plan with strategies and tools that Kaitlyn can use (i.e., getting a calculator, checking in with a friend, signaling the teacher that she wants to check-in) helped her feel confident enough to stay in the healthy struggle. The teacher was also mindful of what tasks she was working on independently and tried to ensure they were within her zone of proximal development to allow her to feel success.

Figure 7.5 *A child gets tape to hold down the bracelet string that was making it tricky for her to string the beads.*

I think about this a lot with opening food packages in kindergarten. Kids enter school with a range of fine-motor abilities and some packages are quite sophisticated to open! While we can teach kids different ways to grip the bags, we can also provide tools that might serve as a scaffold. This might look like having scissors accessible to cut open packets of goldfish or a name chart for kids to use as a reference when they want to write notes to their friends but aren't sure how to spell their names yet.

Figure 7.6 *A basket of tools for students to use independently.*

ENSURING KIDS KNOW WHEN TO GO TO A GROWN-UP

One last thing to keep in mind when we think about how we support kids with working through challenges. While we want kids to try problem solving on their own and with peers in the service of becoming independent problem solvers, we also want to avoid making kids feel like they're all on their own or cannot come to adults. This is the difference between a dismissive "you figure it out," and a "I have confidence that you can do this, and I'm here to support you along the way." It can be helpful to be explicit with kids about times when it is important to come to an adult right away. This might be when they or someone else are hurt or something is making them feel unsafe. We want to preserve the relationship of trust and safety while also helping children grow as problem solvers.

A LESSON FOR OURSELVES

Before moving on to the lessons, take a moment, on your own or with colleagues, to consider the ways your classroom and school communities support students in developing problem-solving skills.

- What parts of the physical environment might be impacting the child(ren)'s problem solving? How might you rethink or adjust?
- How might other peers be impacting the child(ren)'s problem solving? What learning might the community benefit from on problem solving?
- What parts of the curriculum might be impacting the child(ren)'s problem solving? Where might there be opportunities to integrate these skills? Is the curriculum accessible, engaging, and culturally relevant for the child(ren)?
- What is the child(ren)'s behavior bringing up for you? How might your experiences be showing up in your interactions with the child(ren)?

GETTING STARTED WITH THE LESSONS

Now that we've thought about some of the complexities of problem solving and some ways we can support children in developing these skills in the classroom, let's jump into some lessons! Read through the "If You Notice..." parts and you'll find some accompanying lessons and ideas in the "You Might Try..." section that might be a good fit. Lessons that are numbered are already created and available in their entirety in the chapter. Lessons without numbers are seed ideas for potential lessons that you might try creating in your own classroom.

If You Notice...	You Might Try...
Children appear frozen or unsure what to do when they need help or are reliant on adults to help them.	• Ways to Help Yourself (Lesson 7.1) • Ways to Ask for Help • What You Can Do When You See Someone Who Needs Help
Children go to adults when they see other kids doing things that they think they shouldn't (this often looks like "tattling").	• Deciding When You Need Extra Help • Figuring Out the Problem • Noticing Problems and Using Strategies to Solve Them (Lesson 7.2) • Ways to Know If Your Problem Feels Solved (Lesson 7.3)
Children struggle to cope with mistakes.	• Ways to Work Through a Mistake (Lesson 7.4) • What You Can Do When You See Someone Make a Mistake (Lesson 7.5)
Children have a hard time persisting through challenges.	• Ways to Work Through Challenges • Ways Challenges Help Us • Ways to Know When to Take a Break • Ways to Encourage Others
Children get stuck when something doesn't go the way they imagined or they don't get what they want.	• Ways to Think Flexibly (Lesson 5.7) • Ways to Share (Lesson 6.4)

Lesson 7.1 WAYS TO HELP YOURSELF

We want to teach kids to be independent, resilient problem solvers, *and* acknowledge that there is a lot that lies between us doing things for kids and them doing it on their own. In this lesson, we break down the steps behind "try it yourself" and give kids practical strategies they can try when they feel like they need help. This gives kids a concrete scaffold to lean on when they're still learning how to be independent problem solvers.

What Are We Teaching and Why?

Today we're going to learn about ways that we can help ourselves. It can feel kind of scary when someone asks you to try something on your own, especially if you haven't done it before. Today we'll learn some strategies that we can use to help us feel more confident in trying things on our own.

One Way We Might Teach It...

Explicit Instruction with Steps or Strategies

1. *Have you ever felt like you needed help but you weren't sure what to do? Maybe you yelled the teacher's or your parent's name over and over, but they weren't available to come? Or maybe you weren't sure what to do so you just sat there with an uncomfortable feeling? Well, today we're going to think about what are some things that we can do in those moments to help ourselves!*
2. *It can feel really overwhelming when you're struggling with something and I know that you can use strategies to help yourself do it! It isn't always easy, but it can feel so empowering to do something on your own. Let's look*

at some strategies we can use when we need to help ourselves: [Show or make a chart in front of class.]

- Try something
- Ask a friend
- Try another way
- Use a tool (ABC chart, poster in the room, scissors)

3. Model what each strategy might look like. For example, when teaching students to try something, you might model trying to write a word and saying *Ugh, I can't do this!* and then say *Wait! I can help myself! I am going to pick a strategy. I am going to try something!* Then model trying to say some of the sounds in the word.
4. *Today we learned some different strategies we can use when we need help. This week, before we go ask a grown-up for help, let's try out some of our strategies! When you try one out will you let us know?*

One Way We Might Practice It Together...

Role Play or Scenarios

Let's try out some new strategies for helping ourselves when we feel stuck. Read some of the below scenarios (or even better if you create ones from your own class) and have students turn and talk then share out what strategy they might use:

- You're trying to open your pack of apples, but can't get them open.
- You're trying to write a word but you aren't sure how to spell it.
- You just spilled your lunch everywhere and are feeling embarrassed and overwhelmed cleaning it up by yourself.

One Way We Might Support Transfer...

Coaching

Be on the lookout for when kids seem to need help but are using the less-helpful strategies (i.e., yelling your name, sitting and staring when a problem comes up, etc.). In those moments, you might walk over to the student and say something like, *It looks like you need help. I know you can do this. What strategy might you use to help yourself?* (Point to the chart.) Work with the student to pick a strategy. You might stay

Lesson 7.1 WAYS TO HELP YOURSELF (*Cont.*)

with the child for a moment and encourage them as they try the strategy and praise their effort.

REWIND

What to do when you realize teaching another skill first makes sense.

- Ways to Notice When You Need Help
- Noticing When You're Having a Big Feeling (Lesson 5.2)

FAST FORWARD

What to do when you want to add in more layers.

- What You Can Do When You See Someone Who Needs Help
- Ways to Think Flexibly (Lesson 5.7)

Lesson 7.2 NOTICING PROBLEMS AND USING STRATEGIES TO SOLVE THEM

Kids can be incredibly observant. There have been many times where I make a small tweak to something in the classroom and completely forget about it, only to have a student immediately notice it upon walking in the next day. In that same way, kids are quick to notice problems. The glue spilled, it's too crowded in the play area, I can't find my jacket. Noticing problems is an important first step. Next, we can build the confidence and skills to not only notice problems, but take action to resolve them.

What Are We Teaching and Why?

Today we're going to learn how we can notice problems around us and think of strategies to help solve them. We can follow the steps of noticing the problem, thinking of ways to try and solve them, and put them into action.

One Way We Might Teach It...

Explicit Instruction with Steps or Strategies

1. **Notice the problem.** *The first step we take is to notice when we have or see a problem. Maybe you noticed someone was forgetting to flush the toilet in our class bathroom or you notice that every day you are forgetting to bring your jacket home. Noticing problems is an important skill. Slowing down when we notice a problem helps us make sure we are clear on what the problem is so we can find a solution that matches.*

2. **Think of strategies to solve the problem.** *Next, we want to think of some ways we could solve the problem.*

For example, with forgetting to flush the toilet, we could tell the teacher, but that wouldn't really be us trying to solve the problem. What are some strategies that you can think of to help solve that problem? Have the students turn and talk and share some of their ideas. Some examples might be:

- Put up a sign by the bathroom door to remind people to flush.
- Talk to the class about why we flush the toilet.
- Have a class job be a bathroom checker.

3. **Pick a strategy.** *Now that we have a few ideas for strategies to help solve our problem, we want to pick one that we feel comfortable trying out. Let's think through some of the options.* Talk as a class about which one they think would be a good place to start. *Okay, it sounds like we want to start by making a sign.*

4. **Try your strategy.** *Now that we've come up with our idea for a strategy, it's time to put it in action.* Model making a sign or having kids create a sign for the bathroom.

One Way We Might Practice It Together...

Role Play and Scenarios

Let's try out some new strategies for noticing problems and using strategies to solve them. Read some of the below scenarios (or even better if you create ones from common problems that come up in your own class) and have students turn and talk then share out what strategy they might use:

- It's too noisy in the classroom and hard to focus.
- People are leaving the caps off glue and markers and they're all drying out.
- People are getting into fights during recess.
- People are leaving trash on the floor.

One Way We Might Support Transfer...

Coaching

When you notice kids are coming to you about a problem, you might say something like, *You've already done the first step! You noticed the problem. Now, let's look at the chart and see if we can do the next steps and come up with some strategies to solve the problem together.* Encourage the student to remain in the position of the strategy

Lesson 7.2 NOTICING PROBLEMS AND USING STRATEGIES TO SOLVE THEM (*Cont.*)

finder. Use coaching questions like, *What might help?* or *How have you solved problems before? Could those strategies work here?*

REWIND

What to do when you realize teaching another skill first makes sense.

- Naming the Problem
- Ways to Solve Problems

FAST FORWARD

What to do when you want to add in more layers.

- Ways to Know If Your Problem Feels Solved (Lesson 7.3)
- Ways to Think Flexibly (Lesson 5.7)

Lesson 7.3 WAYS TO KNOW IF YOUR PROBLEM FEELS SOLVED

This lesson developed from a noticing I had every time I would pick my kindergarteners up from lunch. As I walked into the cafeteria, they'd begin to list off all of the things that came up at lunch. "Katie said a bad word." "Jonathan ate my chips!" "Harry forgot his lunch." My instructional assistant, Eric, who stayed with them during lunch, would often come over and say, "We already talked about this." As we talked more, I learned that the issues had in fact been resolved. The instructional assistant reminded Katie that we don't say bad words at school, Jonathan apologized to Zack for eating his chips, and Harry had gone with a friend to the gym to get his lunch. So why did they feel the need to recount the details to me? For some kids, I think there was a misconception around what should happen after a problem. Was the end goal to restore peace? Ensure everyone's feelings were heard? Make reparations? Or get the other student "in trouble" with the teacher?

What Are We Teaching and Why?

Today we're going to learn how to check and see if our problem feels solved. This can help us know if we need to keep talking and working on a problem, or if we're ready to move on.

One Way We Might Teach It...

Explicit Instruction with Steps or Strategies

1. *We've been learning recently about how to solve problems. This might look like using a timer to share a new toy or asking someone for help cleaning up our stuff after they knocked into our backpack. One thing we want to think about is after we've tried a solution—does our problem feel solved?*

2. *One way we can do that is to ask ourselves, Does the problem feel solved? For example, if someone was running and knocked into my backpack I would feel annoyed. If I asked them to stop and help me clean up, and they did, I would feel like it was fixed. If I asked them to stop and help me and they just kept running, I*

would feel mad and like my problem was not solved!

- *Think about the problem*
- *Ask yourself: Does the problem feel solved?*
- *If yes → keep going! If no → Try another strategy or get help*

3. *Let's try this out this week. After we have a problem and try a strategy, think about how you're feeling about the problem. Does it feel solved? If our problem feels solved, then we don't need to worry about it anymore. If it doesn't feel solved, we want to go back and try another strategy.*

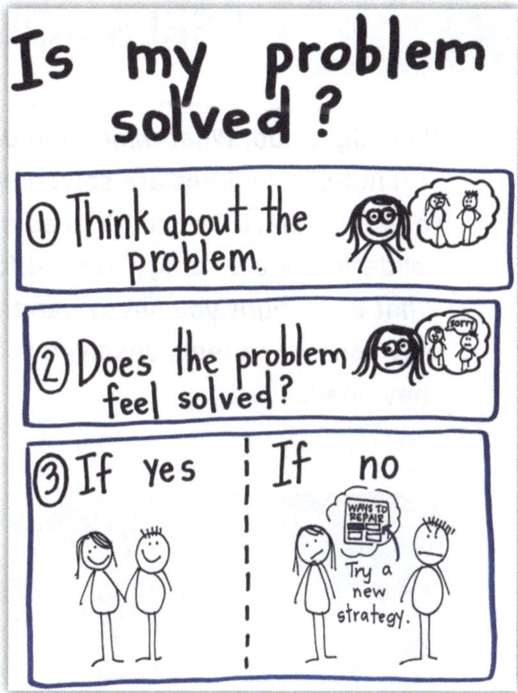

One Way We Might Practice It Together...

Role Play and Scenarios

Let's try out some new strategies for ways to know if our problems feel solved. Read some of the below scenarios (or even better if you create ones from your own class with common problems you're noticing kids tell you about) and have students turn and talk then share out what strategy they might use:

- A student drew on another student's work. They apologized and erased the paper.
- Your backpack ripped and you tried to fix it, but everything is still falling out of it.
- A student is mad that they couldn't sit by their friend at lunch. They yelled for the other kids to move over, but they didn't move.

One Way We Might Support Transfer...

Coaching

Be ready with coaching language for when students come up to you talking about a problem that occurred. You might just prompt them with, *Does your problem feel solved?*

Lesson 7.3 WAYS TO KNOW IF YOUR PROBLEM FEELS SOLVED (*Cont.*)

You might add, *What might you do or try next?* It can be helpful to ask this both when you notice problems are solved *and* when they aren't. This coaching helps build the reflection piece for students as a habit. Sometimes kids might be looking for emotional validation or a strategy worked for one party but not the other. Asking questions like, *What else might you need?* can help tease out what else might be playing a part in why something feels unsolved to a child and give the child agency to articulate what they need.

REWIND

What to do when you realize teaching another skill first makes sense.

- Ways to Solve Problems
- Noticing Problems and Using Strategies to Solve Them (Lesson 7.2)

FAST FORWARD

What to do when you want to add in more layers.

- Ways to Find a Solution That Everyone Is Okay With

Lesson 7.4 WAYS TO WORK THROUGH A MISTAKE

While I know many people with a growth mindset who believe in the benefits of making mistakes, I wouldn't say I know many people, if any, who *enjoy* making a mistake. It is one thing to know the logic of how mistakes help our brains grow and provide opportunities for new learning. And it can *still* be really hard to not feel like you did something wrong. There's a lot of negative self-talk that can creep in when "mistakes" are involved. For some children (and adults!) mistake-making can bring out a lot of emotions and sometimes dysregulation. For students who become dysregulated when they make a mistake, I'd recommend starting by teaching some of those regulation strategies as a first step and *then* introducing skills for working through mistakes. For those who are ready, we can teach them to check in with themselves and then take action to work through the mistake.

What Are We Teaching and Why?

Today we're going to learn about ways we can help ourselves when we make a mistake. Mistakes help us in many ways, but *that doesn't mean they're easy to work through. We'll learn some strategies we can use to work through the uncomfortable feelings that can come up when we make a mistake.*

One Way We Might Teach It...

Explicit Instruction with Steps or Strategies

1. *The first thing that can help us when we make a mistake is to check in with ourselves. What might we need for ourselves first? This could be a deep breath, some positive self-talk, or even a little space before we try to work through the mistake. Check in with yourself first before you act. For example, when I was writing the big sign to go over our name project outside, I was distracted and started writing 'name problem' instead of 'name project'. I was so frustrated because it was on the big, nice poster paper and I didn't want to waste it. I started saying to myself* why did you do that!!! *and that was making me feel worse. I stopped and asked myself, what do you need? I realized I needed to take a deep breath and remind myself* mistakes are normal. You are human. *Once I did that, I felt ready to tackle my mistake.*

2. *Once you feel ready to work through a mistake you can think about some of these strategies to help you.* Talk through each strategy and what that might look like in different scenarios. [Show or make a chart in front of class.]

   - Try it another way (erase and redo, rebuild with a different strategy).
   - Try and turn it into something else (think *Beautiful Oops* here)
   - Start fresh (new paper, cover it with boo boo tape)
   - Ask for help
   - Think about what you learned
   - Take a break

   For me when I had messed up the big sign, I decided I wanted to try and start fresh. I ended up getting some white construction paper and gluing it onto the problem *word and rewriting* project *over it. It didn't look perfect, but I reminded myself that that was okay.*

3. *Checking in with myself first and giving myself what I needed to feel ready to solve my problem was really helpful. Having a choice of some different ways to help me fix it also made me feel less alone. Have you ever had someone say,* it's not a big deal *or* just try again *and felt worse? That's happened to me before. Hopefully using these strategies can give you some more choices and ideas when you feel stuck.*

One Way We Might Practice It Together...

Interactive Read-Aloud

Today we're going to read a book called Beautiful Oops *by Barney Saltzburg. This book is all about how you can take something that first feels like a mistake or an "oops!" and turn it into something beautiful.* Stop throughout the book and consider asking some of the following questions, having students turn and talk with a partner and then share out to the class:

- Before reading: *Think of a time when you made a mistake when you were working on something. What did you do?*

Lesson 7.4 WAYS TO WORK THROUGH A MISTAKE (*Cont.*)

- During reading: *What are you noticing about how they are changing the mistake? What might they be telling themselves when they're doing this?*
- After reading: *This really reminds me of that strategy, "try and turn it into something else." When are times you might try this strategy, or the "beautiful oops" strategy out? When are times when you might not use it?*

One Way We Might Support Transfer...

Pre-conference

Pay close attention to times when you're noticing kids are getting stuck or feeling overwhelmed by making mistakes. For many of my classes it was during art or writing time. There was something about the concreteness of putting something on paper that made mistakes feel permanent and extra overwhelming. This turned out to be a great time to pre-conference and practice utilizing our strategies before we got to work. This might sound like rereading your chart together before writing and even having mini charts close by on tables. You might choose to go over a few relevant scenarios like *You decided to try drawing a tiger today! Parts of that might feel tricky. What can you do if you make a mistake when you're drawing?* This can feel like a little booster shot going into a writing or drawing workshop, keeping those strategies close by in their minds.

REWIND

What to do when you realize teaching another skill first makes sense.

- Noticing When You're Having a Big Feeling (Lesson 5.2)
- Ways Challenges Help Us

FAST FORWARD

What to do when you want to add in more layers.

- What to Do When You Can't Fix a Mistake

Lesson 7.5 WHAT YOU CAN DO WHEN YOU SEE SOMEONE MAKE A MISTAKE

One year I had a student, Max, who really struggled with making mistakes. He'd get really frustrated and start to shut down whenever he perceived that he did something wrong. That same year, I had a group of students who were quick to criticize when students made a mistake. It was the perfect storm. If a student wrote a letter backward on the board, they were the first to say "That's not how you write that letter!" When a student would pronounce a word incorrectly, they would erupt in snickers. Often, we jump straight into teaching the Maxes the new skill. *And* it is just as important to teach the other students the skill of empathizing and understanding how to support others.

What Are We Teaching and Why?

Sometimes when we make a mistake it feels like no big deal, while other times it can feel so frustrating. Sometimes it feels even worse if we make a mistake in front of other people. Even though mistakes help us grow and everyone makes mistakes, it can still feel embarrassing. Today we're going to learn about how we can empathize and help build others up instead of tearing them down when they make a mistake. We can treat people the way we would want them to treat us if we made a mistake.

One Way We Might Teach It...

Class Conversation

1. *Let's think about a time you made a mistake in front of other people. How did you feel?* Have kids share how they felt. *I remember a time when I got to a meeting and had forgotten all the materials I needed for my presentation. I was so embarrassed. In that moment, the other people in the meeting had a choice. They could have shamed me and laughed or said, "I can't believe you forgot that." Instead, they built me up. One teacher looked at me and said, "It's okay! We all forget things." Another teacher offered to go back and get the materials for me. In a moment when I was feeling really down on myself it was so helpful to have someone try and help me out.*

2. *Let's come up with some strategies together that we can use when we see one of our friends making a mistake.* Have students share out strategies that have helped

them in the past or think about what would make them feel good. [Make a chart with their ideas as they share out]. Some ideas are:

- Say encouraging words ("You can do it!")
- Give them time to figure it out
- Offer to help
- Stand up for them if someone is not being helpful

3. *Let's keep these strategies in mind. When we see a friend make a mistake, let's work to build them up and treat them how we'd want to be treated when we make a mistake. We can also help hold each other accountable to this. If you see a friend laughing or not making a helpful choice when someone makes a mistake, help remind them of what they could do instead.*

One Way We Might Practice It Together...

Social Story

One way you might increase the practice and support for specific students with this skill is to make a social story. See the examples in Figures 3.13 and 3.14 for what these social stories that kids can return to again and again might look like. A sample story might sound like:

Everyone makes mistakes.

It can feel embarrassing to make a mistake, especially in front of other people. It can feel worse if people laugh, make fun, or say mean things.

I can think about what it feels like to make a mistake in front of others.

I can say something encouraging, give them time to figure it out, offer to help, or not say anything. I can treat other people how I'd want to be treated.

Lesson 7.5 WHAT YOU CAN DO WHEN YOU SEE SOMEONE MAKE A MISTAKE (*Cont.*)

One Way We Might Support Transfer...

Pre-Conference

Think about times when the class is doing something together as a group and kids might make a mistake publicly. Talk through how they'd want to be treated and supported if that happens. Talk through how you'd want to be treated and supported if that happened. This might sound like *We're about to start our number talk for math. It can feel scary to be vulnerable and share your thinking. What are some ways we can show that we're a supportive class community when people share their answers and ideas?* Reference the chart the class created together and have kids pick out which way they might support their friend if a mistake happens.

REWIND

What to do when you realize teaching another skill first makes sense.

- Recognizing Emotions in Ourselves and Others (Lesson 5.1)
- Ways to Help Someone Having a Big Feeling

FAST FORWARD

What to do when you want to add in more layers.

- Ways to Stand Up for Others
- Ways to Notice When a Friendship Isn't Feeling Good

Chapter 8

Agency—"You're Not the Boss of Me"

We were a few weeks into the school year and I had a student, Jonathan, who was increasingly sharing that he didn't enjoy the structure of the school day. He didn't like that he was supposed to sit on the B square instead of the J square on the ABC carpet; he didn't like that his new race car scissors were added to the communal bin instead of his own; and he didn't like that the toys that surrounded the room had rules for when they could come out. He shared that he despised our schedule, especially reading and writing and that school was in fact, *not* fun. While Jonathan was trying to figure out where he could gain some control throughout his day, he revealed his expert negotiator skills. "I'll come to the carpet if you give me candy" or "I'll write if I get to sit in your chair." The demands continued to grow and when they were not met, Jonathan would make sure we understood his disappointment.

One especially tricky day, Jonathan was in the classroom screaming that we weren't the boss of him and slowly knocking things over and ripping things off the wall while making direct eye contact with the adults in the room. We had transitioned to his least favorite subject, reading, and Jonathan's bartering was not being met in the way he had hoped. He eventually went with another teacher for a break in an effort to regulate and deescalate the situation. A little while later I was at recess with the class and saw Jonathan walking away from the teacher he was with. He quickly took off into the neighborhood. He refused to slow down or engage with us so we followed him closely until we finally got to a nearby cul-de-sac where he plopped down on the edge of a driveway. Hearing a dog barking, Jonathan turned toward us and shouted, "That's my dog Jack barking at you!" It was then that I looked up and realized we were in fact at his house. Day after day Jonathan had been asking us to bend and give him more autonomy in his school day and when he felt his requests had gone unheard, he retreated to a place where he felt like he did have power.

CRIES FOR FREEDOM

When you look up *defiance* in the dictionary, you'll see it surrounded by words like *challenge*, *resist*, and *dare*. These are the same words I often use when I teach my kindergarteners about influential people throughout history and today, and yet when linked to behaviors in school, the connotation associated with defiance changes from admirable to problematic. We encourage kids to stand up for themselves, to say no, to speak up against injustices ... as long as it's not to us adults. We talk about the importance of freedom, but for many kids, schools don't feel like a place where they have freedom. In her book *Troublemakers,* Carla Shalaby refers to the students who cry out about these injustices as canaries in the coal mine, signaling to us the problematic conditions of schools (2017). These kids who bring attention to the lapses in freedom in school are often the ones labeled as defiant. They are desperate for connection and yet these children are the ones who are most controlled and most pushed out of school.

Many people would label Jonathan as a defiant student. In conventional schools, Jonathan would become more and more restricted and monitored, and his cries for freedom and control would get louder and louder. But it doesn't have to be that way. Shalaby writes that schools need to be, "not only a place where young people must be treated as free persons but - more important - a place where they can learn, together, how to skillfully insist on their right to be treated as free people" (2017, xvi). In this way we can see students' behaviors as communication that they need support and teaching about ways to productively advocate for their peers and their own freedom.

When we, his teachers, chose to sit next to Jonathan, a powerful shift occurred. We learned more about where he felt he needed a voice and we were able to teach him ways to advocate for and regulate himself. Learning alongside Jonathan diffused a competition for a perceived limited amount of control and instead put us all on the same team working on a shared goal of creating a community where everyone feels free.

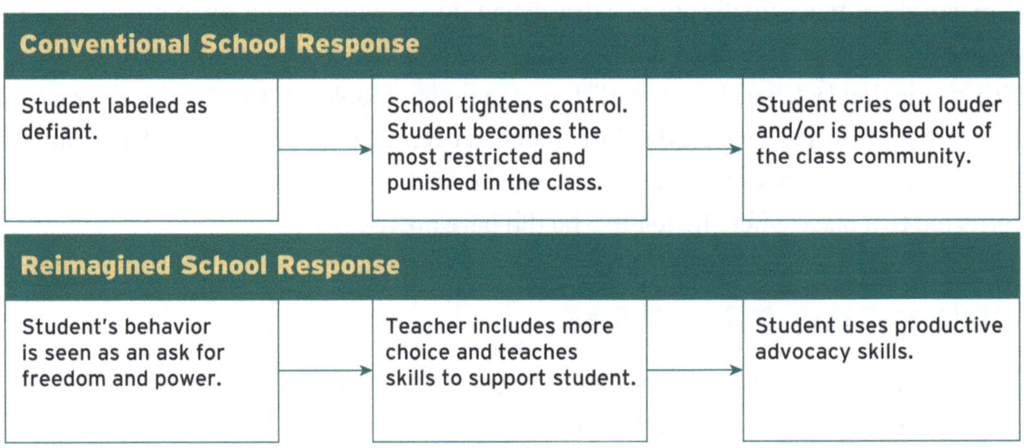

Figure 8.1 *A comparison between a conventional response to "defiance" and a reimagined response to bids for freedom.*

While Jonathan's cries for control were loud, for others they might show up in quieter ways. Children who don't yet have the skills to articulate their needs might demonstrate their unmet need for freedom and control in a variety of ways. In her book *Good Inside,* Dr. Becky Kennedy explains that in this moment when kids are exhibiting defiant behaviors we have a choice. We can view the behavior as disrespectful to us or we can view it as the child having a hard time (2022, 179). I've found it monumentally more productive not to take behaviors personally but rather see the behavior as communicating a need and then act on that need. Figure 8.2 outlines some behaviors that might be telling us a child is asking for more control.

Quiet Bids for Control	Loud Bids for Control
• Staying in their seat when asked to come to the carpet • Wandering around the classroom • Continuing to do something after you asked them to stop • Not engaging in a task • Bargaining	• Yelling "no" or phrases like "you can't make me!" • Throwing things • Hitting • Eloping

Figure 8.2 *We can understand children's behavior as a communication of their needs.*

GRAPPLING WITH WHO GETS FREEDOM IN SCHOOL

It's critical that we are aware that, from the beginning, our educational system has been structured in a way that prioritizes freedom and access for some and not for others. Many schools are set up to value the quiet, compliant students who don't question or make waves. If that is the idealized student, then the student who is loud, moves around, asks questions, and overall doesn't fit into that *norm*, becomes viewed as problematic. These students then become the most watched and controlled. As teachers it's important for us to examine who has the freedom and power in the community. Who are the kids trusted with freedom and power? Who are the kids being critiqued and monitored the most?

FIGURING OUT WHAT'S "OUR STUFF"

I was in a meeting recently supporting a colleague to analyze student behavior. As we talked, she was having a hard time describing the behaviors she wanted to focus on. When I asked her to elaborate she said it was the facial expressions the child made and that they'd whisper to other students. When I asked her to clarify the impact it was having on the child and the learning community, she said it wasn't really bothering anyone … except her. She finally sighed and said, "I don't know why but it gets under my skin so much!" The more we talked, the more she realized that the behavior the child was demonstrating wasn't hurting anyone and it wasn't infringing on others' learning, but more so was just triggering to her. The child was behaving in a way that she wouldn't have.

This might feel relatable, especially if you were a child who learned how to "do school" early on and spent a lot of energy suppressing your wants and needs to conform. As a kid I learned quickly that the idealized student was one who was quiet and compliant. I witnessed firsthand how the loud students who questioned were pushed out and deemed troublemakers. I've had a lot of unlearning to do as an adult. We all have our own unique experiences and when something bothers us it can be helpful to reflect on why it's bothering us and reground ourselves in our core values.

ADDRESSING OUR FEARS

As a teacher it was ingrained early on in both my graduate classes and student teaching to maintain control of my classroom and to "show them who's boss." There was an insinuated fear that you had to maintain order. This fear is why, as discussed in the Introduction, teachers often turn to tools like clips charts and reward jars that shame or manipulate kids into complying. There is a definite fear of losing control and order. But building in places where children can make decisions and feel their freedom is not the opposite of control and order. I'd challenge that students feel more invested in maintaining their peers' and their own freedom. Let's talk through some structures we can integrate to allow for more freedom without letting things turn into chaos.

BUILDING IN CHOICE

The desires to have freedom and control are not limited to children. Think about the last professional development you attended. How would you feel if you were told where to sit, how to sit, what to write with, when to talk, when to be silent, when to get up for the bathroom, etc. Now reimagine you walk in and have the choice of where and how to sit, who to collaborate with, ownership over how you decide to engage with and show your learning? I would be much more engaged in the latter scenario. In her book, *A Culture of Agency: Fostering Engagement, Empowerment, Identity, and Belonging in the Early Years,* Lisa Burman speaks to this idea, writing, "control leads to compliance; autonomy leads to engagement" (2023, 5). Being in control is enticing and the power to make our own decisions increases engagement for adults and children alike. When kids feel a lack of control they can attempt to gain a sense of power in unhelpful ways. One of the easiest ways to shift away from this dynamic is to entrust kids with the power to make some choices and feel like they have an influence over their own lives.

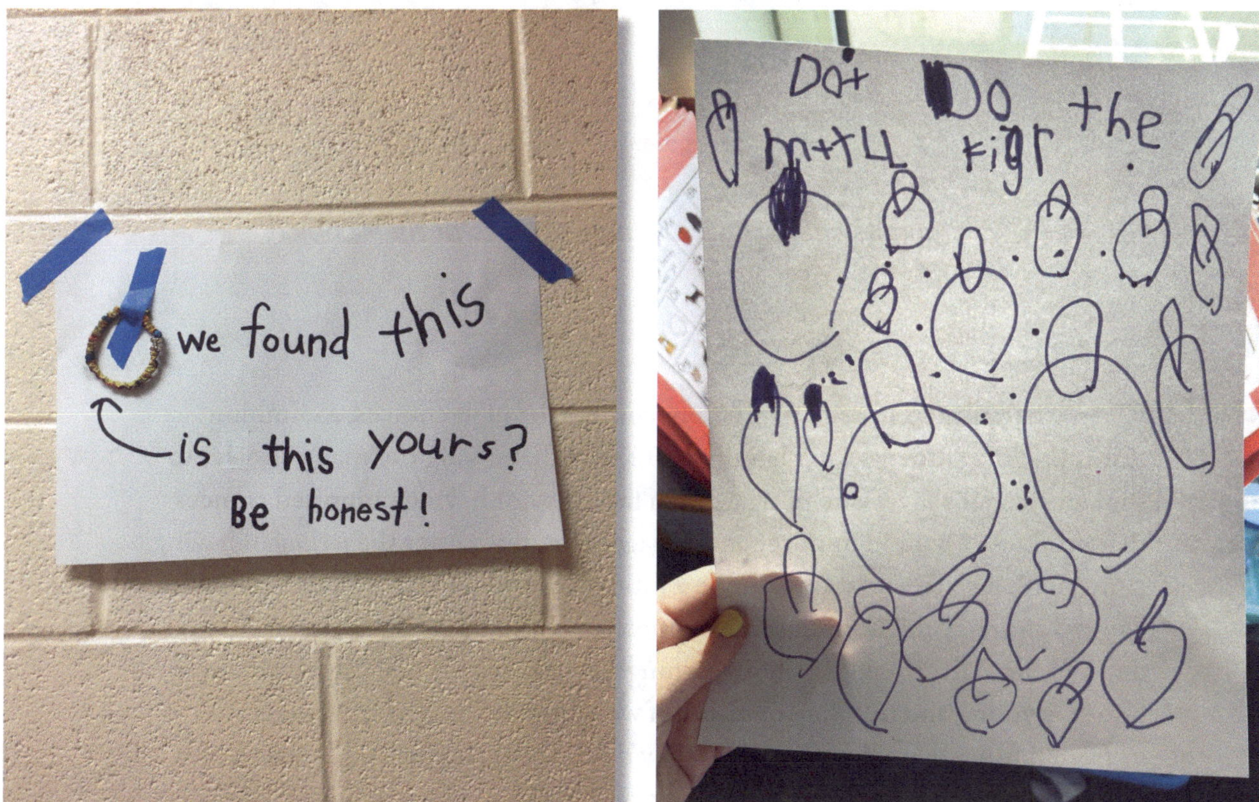

Figure 8.3 *Students take on agency and responsibility in their school community by creating signs that communicate their messages. One sign (left) lets peers know of a bracelet that was found in the hallway and another sign (right) reminds peers not to "do the middle finger" after an influx of this behavior.*

Figure 8.4 *Two students share their writing on topics of their choice.*

STRUCTURED CHOICES

When we think about building in more control through choices, a common fear is that the students can't handle it. It's true that giving too many choices to someone can feel overwhelming. And in fact, it's not having unlimited choices that produces a shift in mindset and engagement, but rather the *feeling* of having control. It's also true that it might be a little messy while kids try out making choices and they might need some supportive coaching, but that's how they develop the skill. Think of a child learning to walk. It's a mess! They're bumping into everything and toppling over. But if we let the fear of the messiness stop us from putting them down to walk, they'd never develop the skill. Alfie Kohn writes, "the way a child learns how to make decisions is by making decisions" (1993). If we want children to learn to make mindful decisions and use their freedoms in a productive way, we have to give them the chance to make decisions in a supportive environment.

It can be helpful to inventory your current practices and analyze where children have the freedom to make choices and where they might not. Reflect on a typical day and note what you as the teacher typically decide and what the child decides. There will probably be instances when it's a compromise like giving two controlled choices (i.e., You can use markers or crayons for this activity.) and that can be helpful to note. Some components to analyze might include: choice of learning content, seating, partnerships, materials, volume, breaks. After writing in the note-taking chart (Figure 8.5), take a moment to reflect on the rationale for your decisions. You might consider these questions as you reflect:

- What do you notice about the balance of decision making?
- What do you think the "right" balance is?
- What impacts how you choose who decides?
- Where might you shift some of the decision making?

Times When the Teacher Decides	Times When the Child Decides

Figure 8.5 *A note-taking chart for reflecting on who is making which decisions in the classroom.*

DIFFERENTIATION

Some things that inevitably come up when we start to bend toward or share control with children are questions like, *why should they get rewarded for their bad behavior* or *how is that fair to the other kids who are doing what they're supposed to?* To combat slipping into this mindset it's important to remember that behaviors are communicating a need. When we look at academic assessments and see a child needs more frequent instruction than other children we don't say, *why should this child get rewarded for not knowing this yet?* Differentiation is common practice with academic instruction, yet when we do it with regards to behavior it can be perceived as giving in or letting a kid "get away with it." Let's remember that differentiation is essential and deserved in both academic *and* social instruction and settings.

LOGICAL CONSEQUENCES

Another common fear is that, in meeting kids where they are and building in opportunities for them to have freedom and control, the classroom becomes a chaotic environment with no limits where kids can do whatever they want. Our aim is not to turn over all control to children and in fact that can feel scary and overwhelming to kids. Instead, we want to provide opportunities for children to make some empowering decisions while they are mindful of their community and shared values.

Consequences without teaching often leads to treading water, and teaching without boundaries and consequences can lead to a skill not being taken on or an environment feeling unstructured and chaotic. We can teach children skills *and* still implement logical consequences. If a child is learning to regulate and hurts another child or threatens safety, that consequence goes in partnership with teaching. Pay close attention to the word consequence instead of punishment (Figure 8.6). A logical consequence is linked closely to the behavior so children make the connection between their behavior and what happens next. Punishment on the other hand is often unrelated and done in a way that produces shame and frustration.

Observed Behavior	Conventional Punishment	Reimagined Logical Consequence
Child elopes from the lunchroom	Loses recess	Has an assigned seat near an adult in the lunchroom for a short period
Child knocks over a basket of books while yelling that she doesn't want to read	Suspended	Cleans up the books and repairs with the person whose basket it was
Child says "no" and doesn't complete any work during writing time	Sent to the office	Works with the teacher one-on-one during choice time later in the day to complete the assignment and problem solve how they can be successful next time

Figure 8.6 *Logical consequences rather than punishments support children's learning and social-emotional growth.*

Figure 8.7 *Students created a closed sign to temporarily close the art center. This is a logical consequence for the time being while they make a plan for how to take better care of the paints.*

WHAT DO I MEAN BY AGENCY?

A core belief embedded throughout this entire book is that there is power in giving choices. Having the ability to choose and make decisions gives kids a sense of agency. You'll notice embedded throughout all of the previous lesson chapters that there is no single right strategy kids are told to use, but rather lots of different strategies are introduced for them to choose from or create themselves. So, what are the lessons in *this* chapter about then? Some of the lessons focus on teaching kids advocacy skills. Things like how to advocate in helpful ways or how to get their message across when they feel like they are not being heard. Other lessons focus on teaching kids strategies to make choices about things many kids yearn for in school.

Oftentimes it can feel a little scary to share some of this choice-making power with children. I remember the first time someone told me about flexible seating and I envisioned kids draped across tables and games of "who can spin the fastest" happening on the wobble chairs in the corner. I knew kids were begging for more autonomy over where they sat in the classroom *and* the actual launch of how to do this felt terrifying. The lessons in this chapter aim to serve as scaffolds for us, as teachers, to try out sharing more of the power in classrooms with kids in a supportive community-centered way. Hopefully the structure of the lessons helps serve as a vision for conversation and teaching around sharing some decision making with kids far beyond these ideas and can be replicated for a variety of other topics.

A LESSON FOR OURSELVES

Before moving on to the lessons, take a moment, on your own or with colleagues, to consider the ways your classroom and school communities support students by cultivating agency.

- What parts of the physical environment might be impacting the child(ren)'s agency? How might you rethink or adjust?
- How might other peers be impacting the child(ren)'s agency? What learning might the community benefit from on agency?
- What parts of the curriculum might be impacting the child(ren)'s agency? Where might there be opportunities to integrate these skills? Is the curriculum accessible, engaging, and culturally relevant for the child(ren)?
- What is the child(ren)'s behavior bringing up for you? How might your experiences be showing up in your interactions with the child(ren)?

GETTING STARTED WITH THE LESSONS

Now that we've thought about some of the complexities of power and agency and some ways we can support children in developing these skills in the classroom, let's jump into some lessons! Read through the "If You Notice…" parts and you'll find some accompanying lessons and ideas in the "You Might Try…" section that might be a good fit. Lessons that are numbered are already created and available in their entirety in the chapter. Lessons without numbers are seed ideas for potential lessons that you might try creating in your own classroom.

If You Notice...	You Might Try...
Children are quietly or loudly resisting doing something(s) throughout the day. You might see them saying no often or communicating their no by throwing things, eloping, etc.	• Helpful Ways to Get Your Message Across (Lesson 8.3) • Recognizing Emotions in Ourselves and Others (Lesson 5.1) • Noticing When You're Having a Big Feeling (Lesson 5.2)
Children are advocating for more choice in where or how they sit. You might notice they get up from their spot often or are sharing that they don't think it's fair they have to sit at their seat.	• Choosing a Helpful Spot (Lesson 8.1) • Ways to be Mindful in the Hallway (Lesson 8.5) • Ways to Work Through Disappointment
Children are advocating for more choice with who they work with. You might notice they gravitate toward others during work time or share their frustration that they never get to work with their friends.	• Choosing People to Work with (Lesson 8.2) • Ways to Include Others (Lesson 6.2) • What to Do When You Feel Excluded • Ways to Work Through Disappointment
Children are advocating for autonomy in doing things on their own. It might sound like "I want to do it!" or them wanting to use different tools than what you are offering.	• Ways to Help Yourself (Lesson 7.1) • Ways to Work Through Disappointment • Ways to Use Special Tools
Children share their frustration around an issue or seem to be pushing back or banding together about something.	• Ways to Advocate for Change (Lesson 8.4)
Children are frustrated when something doesn't go the way they wanted or they don't get their desired outcome.	• Ways to Work Through Disappointment
Children are empowered and engaged when they feel they have a sense of agency and you want to expand their opportunities for choice in other parts of the day.	• Ways to Be Mindful in the Hallway (Lesson 8.5) • Ways to Join a Line • Ways to Choose What You Want to Read • Ways to Choose What to Write About

Lesson 8.1 CHOOSING A HELPFUL SPOT

Choosing where to sit gives kids the opportunity to try out their decision-making skills and often boosts kids' engagement. It also conveys a message of trust that you as the teacher believe in kids to make decisions about where they feel most comfortable learning. This freedom doesn't come without bumps, but remember what Alfie Kohn says: kids learn to make decisions by making decisions (1993). Taking the time to really get clear, as a class, about what it means to choose a good spot and encouraging kids (and yourself!) to hold each other to those expectations is important. And remember, if it doesn't go well the first time you don't have to throw it all away—you just might need to rewind a little.

What Are We Teaching and Why?

We've been talking a lot about how where you sit feels like an important choice for you to make. I hear you. It feels important to me too to have the freedom to choose where I sit. Today we're going to talk about how to know if you've chosen a good spot!

One Way We Might Teach It...

Class Conversation

1. *Have you ever picked a spot, but later realized it might not have been the right one? One time I picked a spot by the classroom library that was so cozy and comfortable, but I was so distracted by all the books that I couldn't focus on my work. Today we're going to think about how we can help ourselves check if we've found a good spot. What are some ways you can tell if you've picked a good spot?* [Co-create a chart with students' ideas as they share out.] Some ideas might be:
   - Comfortable
   - Safe

- Lets you learn
- Lets others learn

2. *Alright, now that we have a guide for how we'll know if we picked a good spot, let's practice. Think of a spot where you might want to do your learning today. Talk with a partner and check and see if that spot is comfortable, safe, lets you learn, and would let your friends learn.* Have a kid model giving it a try and then call on a few others to share how they checked this spot choice with the community guide chart.
3. *This will be our guide to help us pick places to learn. I'll hang the chart right up front so we can check back when we're choosing those spots.* Put the chart somewhere easy for students to see and access. It will be helpful to refer back to it in moments when students are choosing spots or if you notice someone chose a spot that might not match one of the community commitments. You can use the chart to reflect on why and how to choose a different spot.

One Way We Might Practice It Together...

Role Play and Scenarios

Read some of the below scenarios (or even better if you create ones from your own class). Depending on your students you can decide whether you want to have them act out the scenarios through role play or just talk through scenarios aloud together.

- *It's writing time. Think about what your body needs to learn and focus best during writing. Where would you choose to sit? How will you know if that's a good spot?*
- *It's math time and you want to sit in a wobble seat but they're all taken. What could you do?*
- *It's reading time and you find a spot in the back corner. More of your friends come over to sit by you and you notice that you all are quickly getting distracted by each other. What do you do?*

One Way We Might Support Transfer...

Reflection

Watch closely as students navigate selecting seats. Integrate a quick reflection throughout the day to reinforce and problem solve. For example, if you noticed kids

Lesson 8.1 CHOOSING A HELPFUL SPOT (*Cont.*)

chose helpful seats during reading time you might say, *Today I noticed that friends picked really helpful spots. What did you notice that we did well today when choosing seats? How did you know it went well?*

REWIND

What to do when you realize teaching another skill first makes sense.

- How to be Safe in Certain Spots
- Ways to Problem Solve
- How We Can Let Our Friends Learn
- How To Work Through Disappointment

FAST FORWARD

What to do when you want to add in more layers.

- What To Do If You Choose a Spot That Isn't Working
- Ways to Organize Your Materials

Lesson 8.2 CHOOSING PEOPLE TO WORK WITH

"Can we pick our partners?!" It's a question most teachers have pleadingly been asked by their students. And yet—it's tricky. As teachers, we often group students intentionally, utilizing a range of information depending on our purpose. We also likely have experienced scenarios in which we did let kids choose their partners and the work didn't get done, arguments ensued, or students were left out. While I'm not advocating that kids choose their partner for every part of their day, it is an important skill to teach kids how to thoughtfully choose who to work with and reflect on how it went.

What Are We Teaching and Why?

I've been noticing that working with your friends feels really important to you. Sometimes there are going to be times when you have an assigned partner or group and sometimes there will be times when you have the choice to pick who you work with. Today we're going to talk about how we can make a good choice when deciding who to work with and how with that freedom comes the responsibility to make sure you and your friends can learn.

One Way We Might Teach It...

Class Conversation

1. *Have you ever picked a friend to be your partner, but then you ended up talking the whole time and not getting your work done? Or maybe you both were able to focus and ended up working great together. Either way—it's important to be able to notice and reflect on if you've picked a good buddy to sit or work with.*
2. *Let's talk about some ways you might know you've picked a good buddy to*

work with. [Co-create a chart with their ideas as they share out.] Some ideas might be:

- We stay on task
- We help each other (*You're being too silly. Let's get back to work.*)
- We listen to each other (*You're right, okay! Let's focus*)
- We get our stuff done.

3. *The next time you have the chance to pick a partner to work with, think about this guide you can use to make a good choice. After working together, you can use the chart to reflect on if you made a helpful choice or if it might be helpful to try working with someone different next time.*

One Way We Might Practice It Together...

Interactive Read-Aloud

Today we're going to read a book called The Invisible Boy *by Trudy Ludwig. The character, Brian, feels invisible, left out, and unseen for much of the story until a new student, Justin, arrives at school.* Stop throughout the book and consider asking some of the following questions, having students turn and talk with a partner and then sharing out to the class:

- *What do you notice about Brian when he isn't included to play kickball? What could the other kids have done differently?*
- *What do you notice about how Brian tries to connect with Justin?*
- *What do you notice about how Brian, Justin, and Emilio work together? Would you say they picked good buddies? How do you know?*

One Way We Might Support Transfer...

Coaching

After kids have chosen partners and are getting started, walk around and check in with groups. Sometimes our instinct when we see partnerships not working is to take away the choice or make certain partnerships off-limits. If you see a group getting off task, talk to them about it. Brainstorm together what they can do to help themselves stay on task *and* maintain the freedom of choosing the people they want to work with.

Lesson 8.2 CHOOSING PEOPLE TO WORK WITH (*Cont.*)

REWIND

What to do when you realize teaching another skill first makes sense.

- Ways to Talk to Friends
- Ways to Work Together

FAST FORWARD

What to do when you want to add in more layers.

- What You Can Do If Someone Says They Don't Want to be Your Partner
- Ways to Disagree with Friends (Lesson 6.7)

Lesson 8.3 HELPFUL WAYS TO GET YOUR MESSAGE ACROSS

When we think about moments like power struggles or moments of "defiance," what's really underneath is two individuals who have unmet needs. In these instances, both the teacher and the child's message can start to get lost; we can remedy this by working toward clarifying our message and being open to listening for understanding. In his book, *Nonviolent Communication: A Language of Life: Life-Changing Tools for Healthy Relationships*, author Marshall Rosenberg encourages us to, "focus on clarifying what is being observed, felt, and needed rather than on diagnosing and judging" (2015, 3). This lesson aims to help kids express what they're feeling and need.

What Are We Teaching and Why?

Have you ever been asked to do something, go somewhere, or had something happen that you didn't want and yelled "NO!" Or maybe a teacher was asking you to go start your work and you weren't ready so you sat there in silence and ignored them. Maybe you needed a break or some space to cool off, but the teacher kept asking you to start working and you got more and more mad! Those moments can feel really confusing as a kid and a teacher. Our message of what we're feeling and what we need isn't clear. Today I want to teach you how you can help give a clear message.

One Way We Might Teach It...

Explicit Instruction with Steps or Strategies

1. *Think about a time when someone asked you to do something and you didn't want to do it. Maybe your parents wanted you to clean your room or a friend wanted you to move seats. What did you say or do? Sometimes we have strategies to help us work through moments like these and other times we might be having a big feeling and feel a little stuck in that 'no' feeling. In those moments it can be really helpful to communicate a little bit more to help get our message of what we feel or need across.*

2. *There can be a lot of reasons why we might want to say no. We might not feel ready to try something, we might feel dysregulated, we might feel scared. Here are a few ideas we might say when we want to communicate our "no" or "not yet:"*
   - *I'm not ready yet.*
   - *I need more time*

- *I need space*
- *I need a break*
- I need help
- *I feel ____*

3. *Let's pretend it's writing time. You're working hard on an illustration and you're almost done. I call you over to the carpet, but you're feeling so frustrated because you're almost done. You start to feel like you want to scream and throw the markers. What might you say to communicate that you're not quite ready?* Encourage students to talk through which strategy they might try. *When we say a little bit more with our "no," our teachers and friends can hear us better and help us get what we need.*

One Way We Might Practice It Together...
Social Story

One way you might increase practice and support with this skill for specific students is to make a social story. Consider co-writing this with the children. Take a look at Figures 3.13 and 3.14 to see examples of what social stories might look like. A sample story might sound like:

Sometimes when I feel scared or don't want to do something, I leave the classroom.
It's okay to feel that way and it's important to find a safe way to let grown-ups know what I need. When I feel that way, I can use a strategy [*Add picture of chart*].
I can stay safe and tell or show grown-ups what I need.

One Way We Might Support Transfer...
Pre-Conference

Think about a student or group of students who might be working on communicating their "no" in a safe, clear way (this could be a student who is eloping when it's time to

Lesson 8.3 HELPFUL WAYS TO GET YOUR MESSAGE ACROSS (*Cont.*)

go to specials or someone who rolls their eyes and stays at their seat when asked to come to the carpet for whole-group time). Think about times when they are saying "no" in what might be considered a less helpful way and conference with them beforehand. It might sound like *I notice every time we get ready to go to music, you leave the classroom. I think you're trying to communicate something about how you're feeling or what you need. Let's talk about what might be going on. Here's our chart in case that helps.*

REWIND

What to do when you realize teaching another skill first makes sense.

- Recognizing Emotions in Ourselves and Others (Lesson 5.1)
- Noticing When You're Having a Big Feeling (Lesson 5.2)
- Responding to Our Feelings by Choosing a Safe Space (Lesson 5.4)
- Responding to Our Feelings by Choosing a Helpful Tool (Lesson 5.3)

FAST FORWARD

What to do when you want to add in more layers.

- Ways to Work Through Not Getting What We Wanted
- Ways to Try Something New
- Ways to Work Through Something Hard
- Ways to Advocate for Change (Lesson 8.4)

Lesson 8.4 WAYS TO ADVOCATE FOR CHANGE

Why can't I wear my hat at school? Why do we only have one recess? Why can't we get new soccer goals since ours are broken? Teachers know that kids are innately curious and passionate about speaking up for issues and problems that they don't believe to be fair. These qualities are ones that we want to nurture in hopes of creating a world where people notice problems and advocate and work toward change. This lesson helps us equip kids with a process they can use when they want to speak up and make an impact.

What Are We Teaching and Why?

Sometimes we feel like something isn't fair or we don't agree with it. We want to say something or do something about it, but we aren't quite sure what to do. Today I want to teach you that sometimes when we feel like something isn't fair or isn't working, we can advocate or speak out and suggest other possibilities.

One Way We Might Teach It...

Explicit Instruction with Steps or Strategies

1. *Have you ever felt like something isn't fair? Maybe you think that we should be able to pick our seats at lunch or you think that kids should be able to wear their hoods up on their sweatshirts at school. Sometimes when we feel really strongly about something we can consider advocating for a change.*
2. *When we notice something that feels unfair or something that we want to try and change, we can take action. One way you might do this is:*
   - *Decide who you want or need to talk to about the issue.*

- *Decide how you want to communicate with them (send a letter, ask to talk to someone, make a presentation)*
- *Share your concern or why you think something isn't working.*
- *Give them some suggestions.*

3. *Let's try it out together. What's something that's been going on that you might want to speak out about and try to change?* Have students talk with partners and share out their ideas with the class. Decide on one idea you want to focus on as a class. Even if it's something that you think isn't doable to change (like more recess), it's important to let kids experience advocating and the reality of sometimes getting a response that might not be what they expect and then problem solving from there. Go through the steps together.

One Way We Might Practice It Together...

Role Play and Scenarios

Let's talk through some situations together that I've heard you share have been feeling unfair. Let's think through if it's something we'd want to advocate for change on and how we might go about it. Read some of the below scenarios (or even better if you create ones from your own class) and have students turn and talk then share out each step.

- Walking in silent, single file lines in the hallway
- Not being able to choose partners or work spaces in certain classes
- Only being able to check our one library book at a time
- Having assigned seats at lunch
- Not being allowed to play soccer at recess

One Way We Might Support Transfer...

Reflection

I notice that today (and really the past few weeks!) every time I pick you up from lunch you complain that it's not fair that you have assigned seats at lunch. This seems like it's really important to you all. Let's talk through what action you might take to either learn more about why this is a current rule or to share your opinions and advocate for change.

Lesson 8.4 WAYS TO ADVOCATE FOR CHANGE (*Cont.*)

REWIND

What to do when you realize teaching another skill first makes sense.

- Seeing Another Person's Perspective (Lesson 6.3)
- Noticing Problems and Using Strategies to Solve Them (Lesson 7.2)

FAST FORWARD

What to do when you want to add in more layers.

- Working Through Feeling Disappointed
- What to Do When Your First Plan Doesn't Work

Lesson 8.5 WAYS TO BE MINDFUL IN THE HALLWAY

There are certain rules and routines in schools that are so ingrained you'll likely see them in almost any school you visit. Sit crisscross, raise your hand, walk in a silent straight line. And while there are likely good intentions underneath those rules (safety, for example) they don't leave much room for kids to make choices, especially over their bodies. But two things can be true. We can teach kids how to be safe in the hallway *and* give them the agency to choose how they do that. We can do this by teaching the underlying intention of the rules and then collectively deciding how we can uphold those values.

What Are We Teaching and Why?

One thing about being in a school with many other people is that we get to practice considering others. One place where we can do this is in shared spaces, like our playground and hallways. Today I want to teach you how we can move throughout the building by being mindful of others.

One Way We Might Teach It...

Class Conversation

1. *One time I was walking in the hallway and I saw some kids running down the hallway. They were dragging their hands against these beautiful paintings hanging on the wall and some of the pictures came flying down. It made me so sad because I knew the kids who worked so hard to create those paintings and proudly hang them in the hallway would be crushed that someone did that to their work. It made me think a lot about sharing a space together like in a school and how important it is to think about what we value as a class and how we want to live into those values in the hallway.*

2. *Let's think about what feels important to us to remember in the hallway. Picture that our classroom door is open and you're working hard during writing. A class walks by in the hallway. What do you need from them so that you can keep learning?* Have kids share out their different ideas. [Co-create a chart with their ideas as they share out.] It can be helpful to decide on a few ideas as your key values, so you might try grouping similar ones (i.e., you might combine "no running" and "no sliding in the hallway" into "move our bodies safely"). These

values will be the foundation of how kids can "check" the way they're moving about the school, so we want to make sure it's a manageable amount to remember. *Hmm okay so it sounds like we have some ideas for what is important for us to be mindful of while we're moving throughout the school.*

- Be respectful of their work
- Use quiet voices so they can learn
- Move our bodies safely
- Make space for everyone

3. *Now that we've come up with a few agreed upon values, let's think deeper about what those could look like.* Go through one idea at a time. *Which one should we start with first? Be respectful of their work? Okay, let's think through what your body could be doing in the hallway if you're being respectful of their work.* Have some kids share out. Consider having kids draw a picture or take a photo of different options for a concrete reference. If kids seem quiet or unsure, consider giving some scenarios like: *The custodians just repainted the walls and you're walking down the hallway with a pencil. How can you show respect for their work?* Go through each part of the chart to ensure kids have clarity and ideas for each one.

One Way We Might Practice It Together...

Role Play and Scenarios

Gather some pictures of kids in the hallway (i.e., different configurations of kids walking in a line, in groups, running, etc.) and look at them together as a class. Ask students: *Does the way these students are moving in the hallway align with our values? Why or why not?* Another option is to read scenarios to the kids. Here are some examples you might use:

- Two kids are walking next to each other in the hallway. When another person walks by, they scoot over to the side.

Lesson 8.5 WAYS TO BE MINDFUL IN THE HALLWAY (*Cont.*)

- Students are in the bathroom during lunch and are loudly singing a song. The kindergarten class across the hall is trying to listen to a story.
- A student is dragging their hands down the wall in the hallway, but moves their hands whenever there is another student's work on the wall.
- A student whispers to the student in front of them in line that they dropped something from their bag.

One Way We Might Support Transfer...

Coaching

Stay close by when the class is walking in the hallway (hanging near the middle of the line and pausing frequently can help you stay in close proximity to all students). Reinforce when you see students using strategies. That might sound like: *I saw Jeffry take his hand off the wall when he got to that class's poster. That was being respectful of their work.* If you see another class walking in the hallway, you might pause and say *Okay, friends, we have some traffic coming up. Think about what you're going to do with your body to make space for everyone.*

REWIND

What to do when you realize teaching another skill first makes sense.

- Ways to Respect Others' Work
- Ways to Notice and Adjust Your Voice Volume
- Ways to Move our Bodies Safely

FAST FORWARD

What to do when you want to add in more layers.

- Ways to Be Mindful in the Hallway When You're Walking Without a Grown-Up

Chapter 9

"But What About…?": Frequently Asked Questions Around Teaching Social-Emotional Skills

Have you ever been in a professional development session or finished reading a professional book and thought to yourself, "that sounds great but…"? As teachers we often have deep practical awareness, which can come with a healthy dose of skepticism. After all, we're the ones in the classroom actually teaching each day. Over the years I've been asked (and have asked myself) many of the questions that I will have a go at answering in this chapter. Some of these questions are related to barriers, while others consider aspects of social-emotional learning that might not have been previously discussed in the book. These questions, and the "answers" I suggest are meant to be practical and accessible. I hope they give you an idea to try or a resource to check out. Of course, as is the beauty and challenge of teaching, there will surely be questions you have that aren't included in this chapter. I hope though, that you'll finish this book both with a set of strategies, lessons, and ideas you can begin using immediately and with lifelong curiosity around how children develop socially and emotionally and how we, as teachers, can be an important part of this development. I hope this book leaves you with a sense of confidence in your ability to take on both the challenges and the joys of helping children navigate school and the world.

WHAT IF I DON'T HAVE ENOUGH TIME TO TEACH THE LESSONS?

In education it feels like we're constantly being asked to do more with less. Try this new curriculum, implement this new strategy, document this, attend this meeting, go do this professional development; the list of things being added to teachers' plates is overwhelming. As more and more requests get added to the school day it starts to feel impossible to get to it all. This scarcity of time can lead teachers to feel like they have no time to teach social-emotional learning lessons or that they must squeeze these lessons in, delivered to kids and never returned to again. In his book, *Permission to Feel: Unlocking the Power of Emotions to Help Our Kids, Ourselves, and Our Society Thrive,* Marc Brackett writes,

> SEL can't be addressed only in a ten-minute morning meeting or every Thursday, fourth period. It can't be isolated in occasional assemblies for students or in workshops for teachers. SEL has to be an everyday thing- it has to become part of the school's DNA.
>
> (2019, 204)

If you're reading this book, you likely agree with Brackett's statement. You already understand that teaching social-emotional skills isn't just one extra thing to get to, but rather something that can be threaded throughout your day as a core part of your beliefs and classroom community.

But even with that belief and foundation that social-emotional learning should be woven into all we do, there is still the legitimate dilemma of needing time to actually engage in teaching lessons. Over the years I've seen teachers utilize a variety of creative solutions for how and when they teach social-emotional learning lessons depending on their unique situations.

ESTABLISH A DESIGNATED SEL BLOCK

Some schools have designated blocks in their schedule for social-emotional learning. This is a great time to either use the lessons in this book as your core instruction or to use them to responsively supplement your school's existing social-emotional curriculum. Many primary grades also have play or choice time built into their day. This time can be a great opportunity to teach a lesson at the start of the block and then give kids the chance to try it out right away as they socialize with peers during play.

Tell Me More

For more ideas on including play and choice throughout the school day, check out:

- *Purposeful Play: A Teacher's Guide to Igniting Deep and Joyful Learning Across the Day* by Kristine Mraz, Alison Porcelli, and Cheryl Tyler
- *Choice Time: How to Deepen Learning Through Inquiry and Play, PreK-2* by Renée Dinnerstein

INTEGRATE SOCIAL-EMOTIONAL LEARNING INTO MORNING MEETING AND CLOSING CIRCLE

If you don't have a defined block of time in your schedule for social-emotional lessons, then you'll want to start thinking about other times of your day where you have flexibility to integrate it. Many schools, especially if they follow a Responsive Classroom model, have morning meetings at the beginning of the day and closing circles at the end of the day. These are great times to integrate responsive social-emotional instruction. For example, if you notice students having a hard time including others, plan some explicit instruction for your morning meeting the next day. Maybe you'll integrate morning meeting activities where students can intentionally apply the strategies you're teaching them. And then, since social-emotional learning is an all-day curriculum, you can find opportunities throughout other parts of the day to coach and support the kids' independence with this new learning.

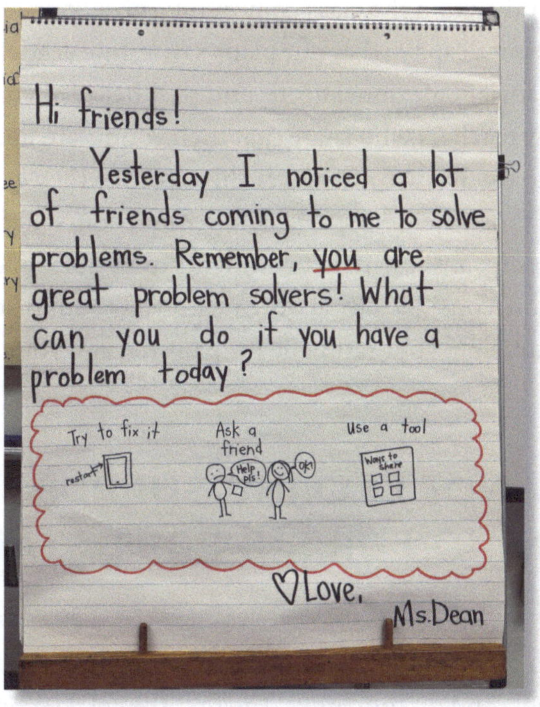

Figure 9.1 *A morning message revisiting problem-solving skills. Students shared ideas as the teacher wrote and illustrated their responses in the bubble.*

ADVOCATE AND GET CREATIVE

If the above options aren't feasible with your schedule, then you have a few options. One is to advocate for social-emotional learning time to be added to your schedule (see more about advocacy ideas in the question about administrator support). If that isn't possible, look at your schedule and see where there might be little bits of time that you could trim down. Maybe work on a tighter transition coming back from lunch that gives you a few minutes. Trim a few minutes off each subject to get yourself a ten-minute block. Integrate two science lessons together into one day so you can use the second day to teach a strategy. Social-emotional lessons don't necessarily have to happen at the same time each day or week. The goal is for our work around social-emotional learning to be responsive and supportive of students' needs. Whatever space we can carve out for the work is good space.

GIVE YOURSELF PERMISSION TO PAUSE

Finally, give yourself permission to press pause. When you notice behaviors bubbling up or there is a rupture within the class community, give yourself permission to prioritize and address it despite what our plans say. While academic curriculum is essential, so are the social-emotional needs and well-being of your students. I've consulted with many teachers who share that their rooms are in chaos and they feel like they're unable to teach any content, yet they feel like they can't stop out of fear of falling behind. In those moments, trust and remind yourself that social-emotional learning and community are essential for students to be able to learn. If you're an ask-for-permission person, consider sitting down with your administrator and talking about what you're noticing, your rationale for pausing, and your intent to get back on track.

WHAT IF I'M NOT FEELING SUPPORTED BY ADMINISTRATION OR SUPPORT STAFF WITH THIS WORK?

This is a really tough one. Teaching is hard on its own, but layering on a lack of support can feel lonely and discouraging. The first thing I'd recommend is finding your "marigolds." The concept of finding your marigolds comes from educator Jennifer Gonzalez, and builds upon the idea that gardeners plant marigolds near other plants because they protect and encourage other plants to grow strong and flourish (2013). Gonzalez relates this concept to new teachers, encouraging them to find their marigold colleagues who support and encourage them. I remember starting at a new school as a fourth-year teacher and sobbing in my room with the door closed one day after the kids had left. There were so many needs in my class and it was starting to feel increasingly out of control. I wasn't sure how to support my students. As I sat at my table crying, I saw multiple faces appear in the little window on my door. My colleagues, and now dear friends, were there that day and every day after to pick me up, validate how hard this career is, and support me in thinking through ways to support my kids. We still have a group chat to this day where one of us will share about something we need support with and the rest of us will validate and problem solve together. We share professional books, podcasts, and continue to stretch each other as educators. I'm forever grateful for my marigolds. If you don't have marigolds in your building, consider other ways to connect such as social media or educational conferences on topics you're passionate about.

Now that we've considered building your own support and growth system, let's think through the day-to-day reality of feeling unsupported. There are a variety of reasons why teachers might feel unsupported by administrators or other colleagues: lack of emotional validation for difficult circumstances, differing beliefs about social-emotional learning or classroom management, lack of response during crises, etc. What support feels like is unique to each individual. In these moments, I think of Brené Brown, author and fierce advocate for having difficult conversations, and her phrase, "clear is kind" (2018, 48). The clearer we can describe the current state of an issue, the clearer we can articulate our expectations and responses to others, and the clearer we can name what support looks like for all parties involved, the more productive our communication will be. When you notice you're feeling unsupported, reach out and schedule a meeting with your administration. Here are a few strategies that can hopefully help the conversation feel productive.

KEEP THE FOCUS ON THE CHILDREN

While it's valid to express your feelings and hear how others are feeling, we want to ensure that the children stay at the center of our conversations. This might sound like requesting or starting a meeting by saying, "Today I want us to talk about the best ways we can support [child or children's name(s)] and keep our focus on them." If you notice the conversation straying away from the child/ren, encourage the group to refocus on them and their current needs.

BRING DATA!

Whether you are meeting to discuss something impacting your entire class or one child, data can be a grounding point for a conversation. This might include data related to behaviors, the impact of current strategies tried, data on academics missed due to behavior, time intervals of behaviors, really anything that supports what you're noticing or advocating for. Data can help bring the reality of what is happening in the classroom to light in a more concrete way. For example, if a child's behaviors are resulting in the class having to evacuate the classroom and you're looking to establish a supportive plan for all of the kids, bring data with the number of incidents and how much learning time the students have missed.

COME WITH A PLAN (OR AT LEAST IDEAS)

I'm sure many of us have sat in meetings that devolved into venting sessions or "we could..." meetings where a laundry list of ideas are shared, but the meeting ends before we have a concrete action plan. To help avoid these unproductive meetings, set a clear purpose and outcome for the meeting (this means you'll want to be clear about your intended outcome before going into the meeting). Before coming to the meeting, brainstorm ideas for next steps. It can be helpful to talk with a colleague(s) and brainstorm ideas together beforehand. You might start by considering these questions:

- What is the data showing the student(s) might need more support with?
- What are you committing to try in the classroom?
- What outside support might the student(s) need?
- What boundaries and consequences need to be created or revised?
- Is a safety or crisis plan needed? If so, what needs to be included?
- When will you meet again to check in on progress?

You don't necessarily have to come to a meeting with an answer to each question, but it's helpful to have some ideas and wonderings to propose and discuss. As much as possible, go into the meeting with an open mind to the different ideas and perspectives that administrators and support staff will bring. Hopefully, through collaboration and keeping the child as the focus, you can leave feeling like you are all on a similar page.

ASK FOR SUPPORT FROM TRUSTED COLLEAGUES

In some situations, conversations with administrators and support staff can feel uncomfortable and it's important to note that sometimes teachers do not feel safe enough to have these conversations, especially when there is a power imbalance between attendees. In those moments you might consider recruiting a trusted colleague to join you or reaching out to other resources at your school and district level such as guidance counselors and social workers to support you with next steps.

WHAT IF I'M NOT SEEING KIDS TAKING ON THE SKILLS I'M TEACHING?

When Carla Shalaby, author of *Troublemakers: Lessons in Freedom from Young Children at School*, came to talk to our school staff, she shared that the school she is supporting is not free of behavior challenges nor is it her goal to create a utopia. There was a deep sigh of relief among staff when she said this. So often when we hear about a new strategy or way of thinking, it is presented as a panacea. Many boxed curriculums are marketed by publishing companies as a perfect fix. Yet, we know this is not the reality. It's helpful to start by reminding ourselves that this is a long game. We're not aiming for a quick fix (which often comes with rewards and punishments) because we believe in the humanity of children and in teaching them the skills and strategies they need to thrive far beyond our classroom walls.

Knowing that we're not aiming for perfection doesn't mean we don't reflect and revise. There have been many times when I teach a child a new skill and they don't take it on right away. In these moments we can reflect on what might be getting in the way and problem solve the next steps. We might even reflect on whether this is the right skill for this child right now. Here are a few things we might try when we're feeling stuck.

START BY CHECKING IN WITH THE CHILD

Teaching skills and strategies should not be something done *to* children, but rather *with* children. We can learn so much from simply sitting with a child for a moment and sharing what we notice and then truly listening. It might sound like, "Hey, I know we've been learning some different strategies we can use when we're having a big feeling and I've been noticing you haven't been using them. Can you talk to me about what's going on? What strategies would feel helpful to you?" Leading with curiosity and a gentle, safe tone is essential here. In conversations with children that I've had over the years when things weren't "working" right away, they shared that they didn't like a strategy, felt uncomfortable using them in front of peers, preferred a different strategy that they didn't know if they could use, and many more things I hadn't considered prior to asking them. Hearing from the child about what was going on helped us to collaborate and tweak things to better enable them to utilize strategies to help themselves.

TAP INTO REWIND SKILLS

I remember attempting to teach a student how to work through making a mistake. I had created and laminated a beautiful strategy chart and was convinced this would support him with the daily eruptions of big feelings during writing workshop. I'd show him the chart I made, eager to coach him through choosing a strategy, and he would throw the chart and kick over his chair. The chart and my attempts to coach my student weren't working. In those moments he was showing me that there were some prerequisite skills (like regulation) that I needed to support him with first before we dug into working through making mistakes. Sometimes we need to teach a different foundational skill first. Check out the Rewind section of each lesson in this book for ideas on what some of those skills might be.

INCREASE SUPPORT, DECREASE TRIGGERS

Sometimes when we're not taking on new skills or strategies, it's because the skill is outside of our zone of proximal development. The new skill is too hard to feel successful with right now. The first thing we can do is increase our amount of support. As a teacher, this might mean doing more modeling, providing more visuals to make the strategies more concrete, and creating more opportunities for students to practice with support. We can also support the learning of new skills by decreasing triggers. While we don't want to eliminate all uncomfortable scenarios that would give the child an opportunity to try a strategy, sometimes we get overloaded when we are presented with an abundance of scenarios. For example, when I had a student who was often in a crisis state and would frequently elope from the classroom, we tried to decrease any other demands placed on her in an effort to help her feel safe enough to try out a regulation strategy. We temporarily removed any academic demands and collaborated with her on creating safe spaces in the classroom. This quickly allowed her to feel available to try out regulation strategies and feel safe enough to stay in the room. As she became more comfortable using strategies to self-regulate, we were able to gradually introduce more academic "demands" and she continued to be successful.

WHAT IF OTHER ADULTS WHO SUPPORT THE STUDENT(S) AREN'T ON THE SAME PAGE AS ME?

Everyone has their own unique set of beliefs based on their own experiences. To some, the most important part of education is to get good grades. Others might place high value on being kind and building character. To others, showing respect to adults might be of utmost importance. These values and experiences all influence how we interact with the children in front of us each day. While there is beauty in these various perspectives, it can also pose challenges for kids who are looking for consistency. For example, if we're focusing on building a student's regulation skills and have created and practiced strategies with the child on how to advocate and take breaks, yet another adult at school tells them they are not allowed to take a break because it's disrespectful to leave the group, that is going to be confusing for the child and can often lead to challenging behavioral situations and mistrust in adults. Here are a few ways to help get everyone on the same page or at least align strategies in support of a child.

START FROM COMMON GROUND

When you're collaborating with someone, especially someone you feel in misalignment with, it can be helpful to stay rooted in your shared goals for a student(s). This might sound like saying, "we both want [child's name] to have strategies for handling disappointment." Naming the common goal can help avoid a me vs. you dynamic and instead create a more shared purpose for supporting children. You can then add, "let's talk about some strategies we can both use so that [child's name] is receiving the same messaging from both of us."

SHARE YOUR RATIONALE

If you're proposing a strategy or process that is unfamiliar to the adult you're collaborating with, share your rationale with them. This first requires us to have clarity on our rationale. There have been times where I've wished another teacher did something in a certain way, but upon further reflection, I realized it was just a personal pet peeve. Whereas other times, I've thought about practices like teacher language and realized that yes, I do have rationale for how and why this impacts kids. When sharing your rationale, it might look like explaining the thinking behind a practice, while other times it might look like sharing an article or book to give more of the "why" behind our practices. While these conversations can sometimes feel awkward or uncomfortable, they can have a monumental impact on children.

GET CRYSTAL CLEAR ON RESPONSES

In many schools, students are fortunate enough to receive instruction not just from their classroom teacher, but also from specialist teachers such as special education teachers, multilingual learner teachers, instructional assistants, interventionists, and more. While this kind of support can have tremendous academic and social benefits for children, as a classroom teacher, at times it can feel like a revolving door of (wonderful!) adults and specialists coming in and out each day. We also know how important predictability and routines are for kids. Kids might wonder: Will *this* teacher expect or allow me to utilize my strategies? How will they respond if I do this? How will they respond if I don't? Inconsistency can lead students, especially with trauma, to feel like they are unsafe. One way we can help create more consistency and safety for kids is to collaborate with all staff who support the child or group of children.

This collaboration might look like sharing the skill and strategy the class (or individual student) is learning about at the moment and what language and visuals you're using to support students with this new skill. It can also be helpful to talk through scenarios related to an individual or group of children. Discuss the strategies the child/ren are learning and talk through what teacher responses in each scenario might look like. This was particularly helpful for a student I had a few years ago where teachers' responses to him not utilizing a strategy ranged from coaching him to use a strategy, to ignoring the behaviors, to taking him to the office for discipline. This misalignment in our responses created frustration and confusion for the child. By talking through and creating a resource sheet for staff with explicit language and visuals on ways to support the child, we were able to create a more unified, consistent support system for the student.

WHERE DOES FAMILY AND CAREGIVER COMMUNICATION AND INVOLVEMENT FIT IN?

Families and caregivers know their children best and are often eager to share and collaborate when they feel safe and welcomed to do so. As teachers, we have an essential role in how we set up and encourage this type of relationship with families and caregivers. If we follow a traditional model where only the teacher shares information about the child and their progress to the families and caregivers, the relationship becomes very one-sided. The teacher often holds the power in these situations and the family or caregivers can be positioned as the receivers of knowledge rather than true partners. Let's think about some ways we can operate from the stance that true partnerships with families and caregivers are critical to children's social-emotional wellbeing.

LAY THE FOUNDATION EARLY

Before the year begins, reflect on ways to establish a collaborative, safe relationship with families and caregivers. What words might you use and actions might you take to help create these relationships? Listening conferences or flipped conferences are one practice that can help set the tone for a collaborative partnership. In these conferences, families or caregivers take on a role of sharing about their child and asking questions, while the teacher takes on more of a listening role. Here are a few questions you might consider asking to invite families to share about their child:

- What does your child enjoy?
- What do you feel is important for me to know about your child and family?
- How does your child feel about school?
- What are your hopes for your child this year?
- What questions do you have about our school and/or classroom community?

These early moments are especially important for us as teachers to communicate our care and interest in the child as a whole.

It's important to also share about your values and practices related to behavior and social-emotional learning early on. Open House, Back to School Night or class newsletters can be great opportunities to explain why (and how!) you prioritize teaching students skills and strategies over typical rewards and punishments.

News from Room 127

September 27th, 2024

A Note from Ms. Dean

Hi families!

We had a fun week together. We have been learning about what feels important to us in a friend. Consider asking your child who they like to play with at school and what makes them feel like a good friend!

I hope you enjoy talking to your child about the letters we learned and the shapes we discovered!

As a reminder, we do not have school on **Thursday and Friday** next week (for a holiday and teacher workday). Please reach out if you have any questions.

Take care,
Ms. Dean

Our Favorite Things From This Week

(Written by the kids)

- Playing with your friends
- Bowling in PE
- The sand table
- The regulation spot
- School
- Celebrating Lyna's birthday
- Going to the park with friends
- Ms. Dauberman reading us the book *What If Everyone Did That*
- Ms. Dean and Mr. Sorensen
- Doing the hearing and vision test
- iPads
- Book shopping
- Looking at the rain

Spotlight on learning

This week we learned the letters m and s! We learned what they look like, their sounds, and that we can find them all around us!

Learning at Home

This week we started learning the names of different shapes. We went on shape hunts in our environment to find circles, triangles, rectangles, and squares. Consider going on a shape hunt with your child in your home or outside! How many shapes can you find?

Figure 9.2 *Weekly newsletter co-written with children for families.*

BE MINDFUL OF HOW YOU COMMUNICATE

In graduate school and in my early years of teaching I remember being told to "sandwich" sharing bad news or problems with parents in between something positive. This might sound like "Caleb is a really sweet kid. He is not listening at all though and I need you to talk to him about this. I really like having him in our class!" While I understand the intent of not simply calling a family to share a list of complaints about behaviors, these sandwiched conversations can feel inauthentic and confusing. Consider how you would feel receiving a call like this about your child. Now consider what alternative there might be that feels more collaborative and warm.

When talking with a family member or caregiver, especially when a child is having a hard time, remember that we want to avoid unidirectional transmission of information to families and caregivers, and instead build a relationship that includes true collaboration. This might sound like calling and sharing some things we've noticed about a child's behavior *and* asking what the family or caregivers have noticed at home. Share about the strategies you and the child have collaboratively talked about *and* genuinely gather input and insight from the family and caregivers. Share visuals or examples of the strategies you're trying so that kids can take them home with them. Check-in frequently about how it's going—both sharing and asking for feedback.

Tell Me More ↴

For more ideas on building caregiver relationships, check out:

- *Nourishing Caregiver Collaborations: Elevating Home Experiences and Classroom Practice for Collective Care* by Nawal Quarooni

WHAT ABOUT CONSEQUENCES? WHERE DO THOSE FIT IN?

There is often a misunderstanding that by not using rewards and punishments to control students there are no consequences or repercussions for behaviors. Layer this with the idea that social-emotional skills are "soft skills," and a narrative can emerge that teachers who embrace these beliefs are passive and "let kids get away with everything." So where *do* consequences come in? First, it's important to determine the difference between punishments and rewards and consequences. Becky Bailey, author of *Conscious Discipline: 7 Basic Skills for Brain Smart Classroom Management* writes, "Punishments and rewards rely on judgment. Consequences rely on reflection" (2000, 227). When we think about consequences, we want to keep our beliefs about "no such thing as bad kids" at the forefront. The more we can connect consequences with actions, rather than judgments about the person, the better.

We can integrate consequences without dehumanizing children and it starts with considering the intent of the consequence. When we think about consequences, I'm often reminded of educator and author Jane Nelsen's wise words, "Where did we ever get the crazy idea that in order to make children perform better, we must first make them feel worse?" (Charney 2002, 143). Is our intent to support and teach or to punish? Let's think about what this looks like with regards to logical consequences.

SUPPORT STUDENTS WITH LOGICAL CONSEQUENCES

Responsive Classroom ("a student-centered, social and emotional learning approach to teaching and discipline") utilizes three types of logical consequences that, when used intentionally, can be supportive and effective (Responsive Classroom 2018). It's important to analyze our intent before implementing a consequence so that we can ensure we're not just disguising a punishment as a logical consequence. See Figure 9.3 for examples of consequences with a more punitive intent versus a logical consequence with the intent to teach.

Another caveat is that sometimes we implement a consequence as something that happens to the student from us. This kind of consequence can feel isolating to the child and affect our relationship with them. Instead, consider how you position the consequence as connected to shared community values. This helps avoid an us versus them dynamic. When implementing a logical consequence, it's essential that the student understands what action the consequence is connected to *and* sees a way to change moving forward. This is where checking in with the student and reflecting and reteaching comes into play.

Type of Logical Consequence	Unconscious or Conscious Punitive Intent	Teaching Intent
"You break it, you fix it."	The intent is to make the student feel bad for what they did. It might look like this: after seeing a student mess up another student's work, the teacher looks at the child and says "you broke it, you fix it," in a frustrated tone and walks away. This response can feel isolating to the child when they're likely experiencing a mix of emotions and this kind of teacher response can convey to the child that they're on their own to figure out how to fix their mistake.	The intent is to support the student by encouraging them to use a taught strategy on how to repair (if you haven't taught this yet then now is a great time). Ground this consequence in your shared class values. This might look like responding to the same scenario of a student messing up a peers work by saying, "In our class we agreed that it's important to take care of our space and each other. Let's work together to pick a strategy to repair this. I know you can do this."
Loss of Privilege	The intent is to isolate the student or make them feel bad for their behavior. This might sound like conveying to the student that they are losing an item or opportunity because of something about themselves, for example, "You're being bossy, so you don't get to play with the dolls anymore."	The intent is to uphold shared class values. Lead with coaching and an opportunity to try again. This might sound like, "I notice the dolls feel really important to you. One of our class values is to be kind to each other. I'm looking at your friends' faces and they look upset. Let's pause and think about some ways you can use a strategy and talk this through."
Positive Timeout	The intent of the break spot is to send the students to a place away from the group. The teacher is the sole decider of when students go to the space. After the break the student rejoins the group, but there is no conversation or repair work related to what happened and what strategies the student could use next time.	The intent of the break spot is to provide students with a safe place to get regulated. These spaces are set up as places where students can choose to go on their own or with teacher prompting. This might sound like, "Katya, I notice you seem dysregulated and are having a hard time learning and letting others learn (one of our shared class values). Go choose a strategy to help yourself get regulated and then come back and join us!"

Figure 9.3 *A comparison of consequences with a punitive intent and consequences with a teaching intent.*

SET AND MAINTAIN BOUNDARIES

I used to think of boundaries as fortresses that kept people away. As I've learned about boundaries in my personal life, my thinking has changed over time. Instead of keeping people out, I've seen how boundaries can actually be a way to strengthen relationships and communities. In the classroom, boundaries can provide a feeling of safety and strengthen the community when they ensure that our shared community values are upheld.

So what exactly are boundaries? Dr. Becky Kennedy writes that, "Boundaries are not what we tell kids *not* to do; boundaries are what we tell kids we *will* do" (2022, 30). When we think about creating and upholding boundaries in our classroom communities, we want to think about what we *will* do when certain behaviors occur. At the end of the day, we can teach and support kids with developing social and emotional skills *and* they have the autonomy to choose whether or not they will try them out. See Figure 9.4 for examples of implementing boundaries related to class values, as well as the social-emotional strategy to teach or reteach.

It's important to explain to children (or even better, to co-create together) what the boundaries and responses are when a class value or expectation isn't maintained. For example, you might say, "One of our class values is to let everyone learn. To us, that means letting people focus by not distracting them and keeping our voices at a reasonable volume. What do you think should happen if someone isn't following

Class Value	Behavior	Example of Stating a Boundary	Social-Emotional Strategy to Teach or Reteach Afterward
Let everyone learn.	Distracting self and others during independent work time	"When you choose a spot that isn't helpful to your learning, I will choose your spot for you."	We can make good choices about where we learn best (Lesson 8.1).
Be safe.	Hitting	"It's okay to be mad, but it's not okay to hit. When you hit, I will help you take a break from our friends to go get regulated."	Responding to feelings using a helpful tool (Lesson 5.3).

Figure 9.4 *Our class values can guide the way we set boundaries and show us what social-emotional learning we need to continue teaching.*

those expectations?" The more you can talk about and get student input around a boundary before it is tested, the better.

Teachers often share that when implementing boundaries or consequences, power struggles can ensue. In these moments it can be helpful to reground ourselves in Kennedy's quote that boundaries are what *we* will do. So, when you ask a student to move to a new seat because they're distracting others and they say no, you can invite the surrounding students to choose new spaces where they can uphold that class value of being able to learn. If a student is screaming on the carpet while you're doing a read-aloud and they won't move to the regulation spot and utilize their strategies, you and the rest of the group can relocate to another quiet spot in the classroom. Then, later you might revisit the student who had a hard time respecting that class boundary and practice together.

LOOKING FORWARD

At its core, this is a book about what it means to live in community with others on the small scale of the classroom, but also in the larger scale of the world. We live in a time when we, as adults, are struggling tremendously to do this well as a country and as a world community. We live in a time in which conformity is often rewarded and any deviation from the "norm" is punished. And yet, I encourage you (and I'm including myself here) to bravely reexamine what that "norm" is. Who are these conventions, traditions and norms working for? And who are they working against? In some ways, even asking these questions feels like going against the grain. When I walk down the hall with my class of children, in a not-perfect line, with a kid safely skipping and another gently dragging their finger against the grooves of the wall, I feel this tension. Sometimes it's through curious glances from adults, while other times it's more jarring like someone "correcting" my kids by demanding silent obedience.

There will inevitably be times when you're doing this work of meeting kids where they are and giving them what they need that people will question your decisions or give you their (often unsolicited) input. "Well, this is the way we've always done it" or "That kid needs to learn how to behave." In those moments, think back to Chapter 2: "Laying the Foundation" in which we established our beliefs and explored what actions live into those beliefs. When the hurdles feel big and the outside noise feels loud, reground yourself in those beliefs. For me, those beliefs are my anchor and guide. When the outside noise feels overwhelming, I like to scribble myself a mantra or message on a post-it note and stick it to my laptop where I'll see it

Figure 9.5 *A post-it note mantra on Mari's laptop.*

again and again. When I'm writing an email requesting a meeting where I anticipate my advocacy might lead to uncomfortable conversations or me being disliked, I look down at my post-it note and remember why it's worth it. There will always be challenges to this work *and* it's up to us to decide how we'll respond to them.

My hope is that this book is a launch into a new way of responding and thinking about behavior and community. This book is far from an exhaustive list of social-emotional lessons and it is my hope that, as you finish reading this book, you feel empowered to create and experiment with your own lessons that best meet the needs of the kids in front of you. Each year the children in my class are uniquely different. Some lessons feel like urgent priorities one year while others feel unnecessary as the students have already demonstrated understanding of the skills they're teaching. Year after year I tweak and revise my language and methods because just as we hope the students grow as learners, we as teachers must grow as well.

At times in the world, it feels like our efforts to build community, to be a community are hopeless. And yet, the classroom community—communities full of children—are always full of hope and possibility. We can work toward that hope and light in the small moves we make in our classroom and in the moves, we hope that we and our children will make in the world.

APPENDIX A

Teaching Social-Emotional Skills Form

Step 1: Observe	
Behaviors that the child is successful with or serve them in a healthy way	Behaviors that the child is struggling with or that serve them in a maladaptive way
Step 2: Analyze and Dig Deeper	
Step 3: Identify a Skill	
Step 4: Plan for How You'll Teach the Skill *One way we might teach this is...*	
Step 5: Plan for Guided Practice *One way we might practice this is...*	
Step 6: Plan for Transfer *One way we might support transfer is...*	

APPENDIX B

If You Notice... You Might Try...

A List of Social-Emotional Learning Lessons from *Lessons in Community*

Lessons that are numbered are already created and available in their entirety in this book. Lessons without numbers are seed ideas for potential lessons that you might try creating in your own classroom.

If You Notice...	You Might Try...
Regulation	
Children seem unsure of how to work through their feelings or often get into a flight, fright, fawn, or freeze state. This can look like hitting, screaming, eloping, hiding, etc.	• Recognizing Emotions in Ourselves and Others (Lesson 5.1) • Noticing When You're Having a Big Feeling (Lesson 5.2) • Responding to Our Feelings by Choosing a Helpful Tool (Lesson 5.3) • Responding to Our Feelings by Choosing a Safe Space (Lesson 5.4)
Children get easily distracted. This can look like wandering around, talking to others, engaging when others are attempting to distract them, etc.	• Ways to Notice When You're Distracted • Helping Ourselves Stay Focused (Lesson 5.5)
Children seem unaware of their voice or body and how their actions might be affecting others	• Understanding the Difference Between On-Accident and On-Purpose • Ways to be Mindful of Our Volume • Ways to be Mindful of Our Bodies • Ways to Tell Someone What You Need (i.e., space, quiet)

Children are having a hard time waiting (i.e., waiting for a teacher or peer's attention; waiting for their turn, etc.)	• Ways to Wait (Lesson 5.6) • Letting Someone Know You Need or Want Something
Children get disappointed when things don't go their way (i.e., losing a game, not getting to go first).	• Ways to Think Flexibly (Lesson 5.7) • Ways to Cope with Losing • Ways to Celebrate a Win
Relationships	
Children seem lonely, left-out or unsure of how to make friends	• Ways to Make Friends (Lesson 6.1) • Ways to Join in • Ways to Include Others (Lesson 6.2)
Children are having a hard time maintaining friendships or often seem in conflict with their peers	• What Makes a Good Friend • Seeing Another Person's Perspective (Lesson 6.3) • Helpful Ways to Get Your Message Across (Lesson 8.3) • Ways to Share (Lesson 6.4) • What You Can Do When Someone Doesn't Want to Play (Lesson 6.5)
Children have a hard time communicating clearly with their friends. It might sound like "you're not my friend anymore" or excluding others	• Ways to Talk to Friends • What to Do When You Feel Excluded • Ways to Repair (Lesson 6.6) • Ways to Share (Lesson 6.4) • Ways to Stand Up for Others When Something Doesn't Feel Right
Children are concerned about peer pressure and unsure about how to handle big problems	• What Problems Do I Need a Grown-Ups Help With • How to Cope with the Fear of Losing Friends • What to Do When Your Friends Want You to Pick Sides

Children get upset when their friend does something different than them. Their understanding of friendship is that friends need to like and do all the same things	• Ways to Disagree (Lesson 6.7) • What to Do When Someone Is Bossing You Around • Ways to Try Something New
Problem Solving	
Children appear frozen or unsure what to do when they need help or are reliant on adults to help them	• Ways to Help Yourself (Lesson 7.1) • Ways to Ask for Help • What You Can Do When You See Someone Who Needs Help
Children go to adults when they see other kids doing things that they think they shouldn't (this often looks like "tattling")	• Deciding When You Need Extra Help • Figuring Out the Problem • Noticing Problems and Using Strategies to Solve Them (Lesson 7.2) • Ways to Know If Your Problem Feels Solved (Lesson 7.3)
Children struggle to cope with mistakes	• Ways to Work Through a Mistake (Lesson 7.4) • What You Can Do When You See Someone Make a Mistake (Lesson 7.5)
Children have a hard time persisting through challenges	• Ways to Work Through Challenges • Ways Challenges Help Us • Ways to Know When to Take a Break • Ways to Encourage Others
Children get stuck when something doesn't go the way they imagined or they don't get what they want	• Ways to Think Flexibly (Lesson 5.7) • Ways to Share (Lesson 6.4)

Agency	
Children are quietly or loudly resisting doing something(s) throughout the day. You might see them saying no often or communicating their no by throwing things, eloping, etc.	• Helpful Ways to Get Your Message Across (Lesson 8.3) • Recognizing Emotions in Ourselves and Others (Lesson 5.1) • Noticing When You're Having a Big Feeling (Lesson 5.2)
Children are advocating for more choice with where or how they sit. You might notice they get up from their spot often or are sharing that they don't think it's fair they have to sit at their seat	• Choosing a Helpful Spot (Lesson 8.1) • Ways to be Mindful in the Hallway (Lesson 8.5) • Ways to Work Through Disappointment
Children are advocating for more choice in who they work with. You might notice they gravitate toward others during work time or share their frustration that they never get to work with their friends	• Choosing People to Work With (Lesson 8.2) • Ways to Include Others (Lesson 6.2) • What To Do When You Feel Excluded • Ways to Work Through Disappointment
Children are advocating for autonomy in doing things on their own. It might sound like "I want to do it!" or them wanting to try using different tools than what you are offering	• Ways to Help Yourself (Lesson 7.1) • Ways to Work Through Disappointment • Ways to Use Special Tools
Children share their frustration around an issue or seem to be pushing back or banding together about something	• Ways to Advocate for Change (Lesson 8.4)

Children are frustrated when something doesn't go the way they wanted or they don't get their desired outcome	• Ways to Work Through Disappointment
Children are empowered and engaged when they feel they have a sense of agency and you want to expand their opportunities for choice in other parts of the day	• Ways to Be Mindful in the Hallway (Lesson 8.5) • Ways to Join a Line • Ways to Choose What You Want to Read • Ways to Choose What to Write About

References

Ahmed, Sarah. 2018. *Being the Change: Lessons and Strategies to Teach Social Comprehension.* Portsmouth, NH: Heinemann.

Bailey, Becky. 2000. *Conscious Discipline: 7 Basic Skills for Brain Smart Classroom Management.* Oviedo, FL: Loving Guidance Inc.

Brackett, Marc. 2019. *Permission to Feel: Unlocking the Power of Emotions to Help Our Kids, Ourselves, and Our Society Thrive.* New York: Celadon Books.

Brandt, Ron. 1995. "Punished by Rewards? A Conversation with Alfie Kohn." ASCD. https://ascd.org/el/articles/punished-by-rewards-a-conversation-with-alfie-kohn.

Brown, Brené. 2018. *Dare to Lead: Brave Work. Tough Conversations. Whole Hearts.* New York: Random House.

Buchanan-Rivera, Erica. 2022. *Identity Affirming Classrooms: Spaces that Center Humanity.* New York: Routledge.

Burman, Lisa. 2023. *A Culture of Agency: Fostering Engagement, Empowerment, Identity, and Belonging in the Early Years.* St. Paul, Minnesota: Redleaf Press.

Center on the Developing Child at Harvard University. 2011. "Building the Brain's 'Air Traffic Control' System: How Early Experiences Shape the Development of Executive Function." https://developingchild.harvard.edu/wp-content/uploads/2024/10/How-Early-Experiences-Shape-the-Development-of-Executive-Function.pdf.

Charney, Ruth Sidney. 2002. *Teaching Children to Care: Classroom Management for Ethical and Academic Growth, K-8, Revised Edition.* Turners Falls, MA: Center for Responsive Schools.

Collaborative for Academic, Social, and Emotional Learning (CASEL). 2025. https://casel.org/.

Davis, Carol, and Alice Yang. 2005. *Parents and Teachers Working Together.* Greenfield, MA: Northeast Foundation for Children.

Denton, Paula. 2007. *The Power of Our Words: Teacher Language That Helps.* Turners Falls, MA: Center for Responsive Schools.

Durlak, Joseph A. et al. 2011. "The Impact of Enhancing Students' Social and Emotional Learning: A Meta-Analysis of School-Based Universal Interventions." *Child Development* 82 (1): 405–432.

Dweck, Carol. 2007. *Mindset: The New Psychology of Success.* New York: Ballantine Books.

Galinsky, Ellen. 2010. *Mind in the Making: The Seven Essential Life Skills Every Child Needs.* New York: HarperCollins.

Gonzalez, Jennifer. 2013. "Find Your Marigold: The One Essential Rule for New Teachers." *Cult of Pedagogy.* https://www.cultofpedagogy.com/marigolds/.

Greene, Ross. 2014. *Lost at School.* New York: Scribner.

Hertz, Christine, and Kristine Mraz. 2015. *A Mindset for Learning: Teaching the Traits of Joyful, Independent Growth.* Portsmouth, NH: Heinemann.

hooks, bell. 1994. *Teaching to Transgress: Education as the Practice of Freedom.* New York, NY: Routledge.

Kennedy, Becky. 2022. *Good Inside: A Practical Guide to Resilient Parenting Prioritizing Connection over Correction.* New York: Harper Wave.

Kohn, Alfie. 1993. "Choices for Children: Why and How to Let Students Decide." https://www.alfiekohn.org/article/choices-children/.

McClelland, Megan M., and Shauna L. Tominey. 2015. *Stop, Think, Act: Integrating Self-Regulation in the Early Childhood Classroom*. New York: Routledge.

Moll, Luis. C., Cathy Amanti, Deborah Neff, and Norma Gonzalez. 1992. "Funds of Knowledge for Teaching: Using a Qualitative Approach to Connect Homes and Classrooms." *Theory into Practice* 31 (2): 132–141. https://doi.org/10.1080/00405849209543534.

Murray, Desiree W., Katie Rosanbalm, Christina Christopoulos, and Amar Hamoudi. 2015. "*Self-Regulation and Toxic Stress Report 1: Foundations for Understanding Self-Regulation from an Applied Perspective (OPRE Report #2015-21)*." Washington, DC: Office of Planning, Research and Evaluation, Administration for Children and Families, U.S. Department of Health and Human Services. https://acf.gov/sites/default/files/documents/report_1_foundations_paper_final_012715_submitted_508_0.pdf.

Parekh, Gillian. 2022. *Ableism in Education: Rethinking School Practices and Policies*. New York, NY: Routledge.

Qarooni, Nawal. 2024. *Nourishing Caregiver Collaborations: Elevating Home Experiences and Classroom Practices for Collective Care*. New York: Routledge.

Responsive Classroom. 2018. "The Responsive Classroom Approach." https://www.responsiveclassroom.org/wp-content/uploads/2018/07/RC-Approach-Handout.pdf.

Rosenberg, Marshall. 2015. *Nonviolent Communication: A Language of Life: Life-Changing Tools for Healthy Relationships*. Encinitas, CA: PuddleDancer Press.

Serravallo, Jennifer. 2015. *The Reading Strategies Book: Your Everything Guide to Developing Skilled Readers*. Portsmouth, NH: Heinemann.

Shalaby, Carla. 2017. *Troublemakers: Lessons in Freedom From Children from Young Children at School*. New York: The New Press.

Souers, Kristin, and Pete Hall. 2016. *Fostering Resilient Learners: Strategies for Creating a Trauma-Sensitive Classroom*. Alexandria, VA: ASCD.

Souers, Kristin Van Marter, and Pete Hall. 2018. *Relationships, Responsibility and Regulation: Trauma-Invested Practices for Fostering Resilient Learners*. Alexandria, VA: ASCD.

U.S. Department of Education. 2023. *2020–21 Civil Rights Data Collection: Student Discipline and School Climate in U.S. Public Schools*. Washington, DC: U.S. Department of Education. https://www.ed.gov/media/document/crdc-discipline-school-climate-reportpdf-21409.pdf.

Venet, Alex Shevrin. 2021. *Equity-Centered Trauma-Informed Education*. New York: Routledge.

Zimmermann, Calvin Rashaud. 2024. "Looking for Trouble: How Teachers' Racialized Practices Perpetuate Discipline Inequities in Early Childhood." *Sociology of Education* 97 (3): 219–232. https://doi.org/10.1177/00380407241228581.

Index

Note: Page references in *italics* denote figures.

For Product Safety Concerns and Information,
please contact our EU representative GPSR@taylorandfrancis.com
Taylor & Francis Verlag GmbH, Kaufingerstraße 24,
80331 München, Germany

Printed by Integrated Books International,
United States of America